M000195492

"In these pages, Torvend pushes be〉 communal meanings of the Christian Eucharist to its large implications for social well-being and the good of the earth itself. The worldly ground and horizon of eucharistic practice emerges clearly here through fresh biblical reflections and many voices out of Christian history. Far more than an academic treatise, this is an urgent plea that Christian eucharistic feasting address the cries of the world's hungry and poor, the afflicted and oppressed."

— Thomas H. Schattauer
     Professor of Liturgics
     Wartburg Theological Seminary, Dubuque, Iowa

"Samuel Torvend's *Still Hungry at the Feast* is a beautifully written primer on the spirituality of living eucharistically; living what we pray and praying what we live. Continuing the work of Monika Hellwig and others, Torvend asks 'who is hungry at the feast?' and proceeds to expand that question into contemporary realities regarding the Eucharist as the liturgy of the world in the face of real hunger as well as real capabilities to distribute food equitably. Eschewing the facile trends of the casualness of 'word' and 'meal,' Torvend draws on Scripture, particularly the gospel of Luke, a breadth of early Christian tradition, and his own facility in Lutheran, Anglican, and Roman Catholic theologies and practices to guide his readers toward the reality that every Eucharist is a 'Mass of Creation' rooted in the materiality that God has created and with which we are intimately related. Both generous in breadth and focused in intent, this small book exemplifies the 'economy of grace' in which the author places the Eucharist, gift of God, and work of human hands. May we take into action the 'economy of grace' at the heart of this writing!"

— Lizette Larson-Miller
     Huron University College, University of Western Ontario, Canada
     Author of *Sacramentality Renewed: Contemporary Conversations in Sacramental Theology*

Still Hungry at the Feast

Eucharistic Justice in the Midst of Affliction

Samuel Torvend

LITURGICAL PRESS
ACADEMIC

Collegeville, Minnesota
www.litpress.org

Cover design by Monica Bokinskie.
Image courtesy of Wikimedia Commons.
In ancient Mediterranean practice, women and children were normally separated from the men who reclined at table for a meal. In the Roman catacomb of the fourth-century martyrs Marcellinus and Peter, however, two women, three men, and two children sit together at an early Christian feast. To the left, the artist has written, *AGAPE MISCEMI*, "Love-for-others brings the mixed cup [of wine and water]." To the right, and barely discernible between the woman and the man, are these words inscribed on the wall: *IRENE DA CALDA*, "Peace gives food." Here, in this place that commemorates two Christians executed by Rome's violence, peace and love-for-others surround those gathered at table.

Scripture quotations are from New Revised Standard Version Bible © 1989 National Council of the Churches of Christ in the United States of America. Used by permission. All rights reserved worldwide.

Excerpts from the English translation of *The Roman Missal* © 2010, International Commission on English in the Liturgy Corporation. All rights reserved.

"The Didache," trans. Bland Tucker. From *The Hymnal 1982*, © 1985 the Church Pension Fund. All rights reserved. Used by permission of Church Publishing Incorporated, New York, NY.

Susan Palo Cherwien, *O Blessed Spring: Hymns of Susan Palo Cherwien*. All rights reserved. Used by permission of Augsburg Fortress, Minneapolis, MN.

1   2   3   4   5   6   7   8   9

Library of Congress Control Number: 2018952113

ISBN 978-0-8146-8468-9   ISBN 978-0-8146-8492-4 (ebook)

With love and gratitude for Sean Horner
dilectus meus in fide et vita socium

Contents

Chapter 8

Introduction

By my calculation, I have participated in the Eucharist 8,050 times since I was five years old, a calculation that includes Sunday, daily, and feast day masses. I remember some of them because of the place in which the liturgy was celebrated—the shore of Similk Bay in my native Washington, the Holy Sepulcher in Jerusalem, St. Paul's in Seattle, the Basilica of St. Francis in Assisi, the medieval Selbu Kirke in central Norway, the monastic church of St. John's Abbey in Collegeville. Others I remember vividly because of the events that called for the Eucharist: the death of my father; the day I was married to my beloved; ordination to the priesthood; the Sunday liturgies after the assassinations of John Fitzgerald Kennedy and Martin Luther King Jr.; the huge crowd crammed into our parish church during the Cuban Missile Crisis.

And yet, significant places and significant events have not obscured that dimension to which the eucharistic liturgy invites those who receive bread and drink wine—the ethical invitations and instructions offered in this ancient communal ritual: "Eternal God, you have graciously accepted us as living members of your Son our Savior Jesus Christ, and have fed us with the Sacrament of his Body and Blood. Send us now into the world in peace, and grant us strength and courage to love and serve you with gladness and singleness of heart."[1] In the world of specialization that marks the

---

[1] A post-communion prayer in *The Book of Common Prayer* (New York: The Church Hymnal Corporation, 1979), 365.

academy and much of contemporary life, sacraments and ethics, liturgy and life are usually separated from each other in study and in practice—one of the reasons why the yearning for an integrated and holistic spirituality can be so easily thwarted. Such compartmentalization of Christian faith and life seems more the norm than the exception.

But need it be? For centuries, the fathers and mothers of the church have unfolded the meaning of the liturgy for daily life because they understood that the words, gestures, and postures of the Christian assembly have the power to form the actions of the assembly in the world: *the rule of prayer shapes the rule of living.*[2] Consider, for instance, the mystagogical sermons of John Chrysostom and Ambrose of Milan; the sacramental poetry of Hildegard of Bingen and Catherine of Siena; the eucharistic hymns of Thomas Aquinas; the artwork of Giotto di Bondone and Andrei Rublev; the sermons of Martin Luther and the eucharistic collects of Thomas Cranmer; the writings of Virgil Michel, Romano Guardini, Photina Rech, Balthasar Fischer, Antonio Donghi, and Gordon Lathrop.[3] All of these and many others

---

[2] But before we accept at face value the oft-used dictum about prayer and life, let us note clearly the insightful criticism of feminist Christians who expose the patriarchal power manifest in the use of exclusive language in worship and the rejection of women in liturgical leadership in some Christian communions; the deployment of strategies to limit or exclude the use of musical traditions of cultures different from the dominant one in a parish or cathedral; the use of insipid lyrics in the liturgy that obscure the rich metaphorical tradition across the centuries and across the globe; artwork that communicates racial bias and is historically inaccurate—all of these and more participate in the *deformation of common prayer and Christian witness in the world.*

[3] Virgil Michel, OSB, *The Liturgy of the Church* (New York: Macmillan, 1938); Romano Guardini, *Sacred Signs* (St. Louis: Pio Decimo, 1956/Wilmington: Michael Glazier, 1979); Photina Rech, OSB, *Wine and Bread*, trans. Heinz Kuehn (Salzburg: Otto Müller, 1966/Chicago: Liturgy Training Publications, 1998); Balthasar Fischer, *Signs, Words & Gestures*, trans. Matthew O'Connell (Freiburg im Breisgau: Herder, 1979/New York: Pueblo, 1981); Antonio Donghi, *Words and Gestures in the Liturgy*, trans.

recognized that the Mass, the Holy Communion, orients the worshiping assembly toward its life in the world, a life marked by an ethic of care for other people, their communities, and the earth.

In 1977, the Sri Lankan theologian and priest Tissa Balasuriya, OMI, published *Eucharist and Human Liberation*.[4] In this provocative work, Fr. Balasuriya asked a number of troubling questions that startled readers who found it difficult to imagine any relationship between sacraments and ethics:

> Why is it that in spite of hundreds of thousands of daily and weekly Masses, Christians continue as selfish as before? Why have the "Christian" Mass-going peoples been the most cruel colonizers of human history? Why is it that persons and people who proclaim Eucharistic love and sharing deprive the poor people of the world of food, capital, employment and even land? Why mass human sterilization in poor countries and affluence unto disease and pollution of nature among the rich?[5]

Exposing what he considered the compartmentalization of Christian faith and life—worship directed to the Holy Three yet separated from daily practice in the world—Balasuriya argued that the meal practice of Jesus, soon to be called the Eucharist, soon to be called the Mass, clearly expressed *Christ's commitment to all* who participated in his ongoing table fellowship. But at the same time, participation in *the sacramental encounter asked for commitment from those who participated*—and that commitment "to love one another

---

William McDonough, Dominic Serra, and Ted Bertagni (Rome: Libreria Editrice Vaticana, 1993/Collegeville: Liturgical Press, 2009); Gordon Lathrop, *Holy Ground: A Liturgical Cosmology* (Minneapolis: Fortress Press, 2003).

[4] Tissa Balasuriya, OMI, *Eucharist and Human Liberation* (Colombo, Sri Lanka: The Centre for Society and Religion, 1977/ Eugene: Wipf & Stock, 2004).

[5] Balasuriya, *Eucharist and Human Liberation*, 2.

as I have loved you" was and is confirmed in action: "The Mass," he wrote, "leads us to respond to the suffering of the masses."

While J. S. Bach signed all of his sacred music compositions with the Latin phrase *Soli Deo Gloria* ("Glory to God alone")—and many church musicians since the eighteenth century have been diligent in copying his practice—this one phrase alone is insufficient and misleading. The lexicon of Catholic and historical Christianity, inspired by its central text, the Bible, is shot through with metaphor, with the linking of two images, two words, two phrases: an implicit antidote to the fundamentalist tendency that lurks in every human being. Praise of God—giving glory to God—never takes place in a vacuum. The assembly gathered for the liturgy gathers on this earth, in a particular place at a particular moment in human history. Set next to the praise or worship of God, set next to this acceptable sacrifice, is the suffering of the many and the earth itself. This should come as no surprise: in Jewish and Christian practice, thanksgiving to God always leads to supplication that God act in the present, in the world, with and through the people of God. Indeed, as I write these words, famine sweeps through large portions of the African continent. Species are dying rapidly for lack of sufficient food due to climate change. Child hunger and chronic malnutrition continue in the United States, though political leaders rarely mention the embarrassment of such statistics and the suffering they represent.

Here we ask the question, "Who is hungry at the feast?" To be honest, I think I am. I yearn for, I am hungry for the word, the image, the lyric, and the prayer that will invite many others and me to "redress the terrible injustices, deprivations, and imbalances that surround us."[6] Who is still

---

[6] Monika Hellwig, "The Eucharist and the Hunger of the World," in *Word and World* 17, no. 1 (1997): 65.

hungry at the feast? The many who will never read this text because they must work two or three jobs each day, six days each week, in order to feed their children in a society that rewards the wealthy and stigmatizes the working poor. Who is still hungry at the feast? The people of this world "deprived of food, capital, employment and land."

Here we consider ethical dimensions of this ancient and contemporary practice. There is no prescription, only fragments of words and practices that offer an alternative to the perception alive in many ecclesial communities that the Mass, the Holy Eucharist, is really about this one thing: my personal relationship with the Lord, my union with Christ, my forgiveness of sin. Not so, I say, not so. One word is never sufficient. Set next to this communion is a sharing, an abundance, that extends beyond the assembly and me. The eucharistic table holds the finest wheat and the richest wine drawn from the earth and fashioned by human labor. But the stewardship of these gifts has been placed in the hands of the assembly who live in the world, a world marked by the many who continue to hunger for bread, for companionship, for justice—and yes, for nothing less than life itself.

To these friends and colleagues, I offer my thanks: David and Susan Cherwien, John and Jennifer Forman, Joseph and Deborah Hickey-Tiernan, Doug and Deborah Oakman, Rebecca Torvend Rainsberger, Benjamin Stewart, the Commission on Liturgy and the Arts of the Diocese of Olympia, and the members and friends of St. Paul's Seattle and Christ Church Tacoma. I am grateful for those who have responded to and reviewed chapters or portions of chapters in this book: students and faculty colleagues in Rome who reviewed chapter 1 ("The Worldly Trajectory of the Eucharist"); students enrolled in my course "Early Christian Responses to the Hungry Poor" for their consideration of chapter 3 ("Eating with the Hungry and the Outcast"); and the members of Societas Liturgica, the Liturgy and Ecology Seminar of the North American Academy of Liturgy, and the Department of Religion at Pacific Lutheran University who responded to chapter 4 ("The Banquet of God's Vulnerable Creation"). I am grateful for Christopher Kiesling, OP (+), and his collaboration with James Empereur, SJ, on *The Liturgy That Does Justice*, and for Fr. Kiesling's leadership of the Liturgy and Social Justice Seminar of the North American Academy of Liturgy. I give thanks for the work and support of Ralph Carskadden (+), priest and mentor, who recognized the intimate relationship between liturgy, justice, and the visual arts. And I give thanks for my father, E. Silas Torvend (+), who, with my mother, Alice Kjesbu Torvend, brought me to the altar of God. I am indebted to Sean Horner, whose research and teaching on the economy and the environment have brought fresh insight to the eucharistic mystery. I am grateful to Nancy de Flon for her copyediting expertise. I offer my thanks to Hans Christoffersen, Tara Durheim, Stephanie Lancour, and Colleen Stiller of Liturgical Press for their insight, advice, and support.

Samuel Torvend
August 10, 2017
St. Lawrence, Deacon and Martyr at Rome

Lectionary Abbreviations and References

References to readings in the *Lectionary for Mass* (LM), the lectionary of *Evangelical Lutheran Worship* (ELW L), and the *Revised Common Lectionary* (RCL) follow the abbreviations listed below with day and year. Thus, Adv 1A refers to the First Sunday of Advent in Year A. Lectionary readings for the Sundays in Ordinary Time are listed by lectionary: LM Ord 13C; ELW L 13C; RCL: Pr. 8.

Adv	Advent
AllS	All Saints
AllSo	All Souls
Ash	Ash Wednesday
Assum	Assumption of the Blessed Virgin Mary
Bapt	Baptism of the Lord
CKing	Christ the King
Corpus	Corpus Christi
East	Easter
EastEve	Easter Sunday Evening
Epi	Epiphany
EVig	Easter Vigil

HW	Holy Week
L	ELW Lectionary
Lent	Lent
LM	Lectionary for Mass
NewY	New Year's Day
Ord	Ordinary Time
Pass	Good Friday
Pent	Pentecost
Pr.	RCL Proper
RCL	Revised Common Lectionary
Trin	Holy Trinity

Chapter One

The Worldly Trajectory
of the Eucharist

Now on that same day two of them were going to a village called Emmaus. . . . While they were talking and discussing, Jesus himself came near and went with them, but their eyes were kept from recognizing him. . . . He said to them, "What are you discussing with each other while you walk along?" They stood still [and] replied . . . "The things about Jesus of Nazareth, who was a prophet mighty in deed and word before God and all the people, and how our chief priests and leaders handed him over to be condemned to death and crucified him. But we had hoped that he was the one to redeem Israel. Yes, and besides all this, it is now the third day since these things took place." . . . Then beginning with Moses and all the prophets, [Jesus] interpreted to them the things about himself in all the scriptures.

As they came near the village to which they were going, he walked ahead as if he were going on. But they urged him strongly, saying, "Stay with us. . . ." So he went in to stay with them. When he was at the table with them, he took bread, blessed and broke it, and gave it to them. Then their eyes were opened, and they recognized him; and he vanished from their sight. They said to each other, "Were not our hearts burning within us while he was talking to us on the road, while he was opening the scriptures to us?" That same hour they got up and returned to Jerusalem; and they found the eleven and their

companions gathered together. . . . They told what had happened on the road, and how he had been made known to them
in the breaking of the bread.[1]

Whether they worship in a spacious cathedral or a small
mission chapel, more than two billion Christians throughout
the world follow a common pattern of worship, an order or
ordo,[2] revealed in the Roman Missal, the Divine Liturgy of
St. John Chrysostom, the Book of Common Prayer, and the
books of various Protestant communions. While different
words may be used to describe the pattern, they nonetheless
reveal a fourfold movement: the baptized people of God
gather for the reading and interpretation of *Scripture*, for
thanksgiving over and *communion* in the gifts of bread and
wine, and for *sending* into home, work, and public life.[3]
While a visitor in the liturgical assembly might imagine that
this form of worship comes from a book, leaflet, or mis-
salette, from a priest or a commission, the pattern, in fact,
can be traced to the New Testament, to that encounter between the risen Christ and two of his followers on a Sunday,
the day of his unexpected appearing after his execution by
the Roman imperial army.

A Resurrection Appearance in Ordinary Time

Luke narrates this fourfold movement. A stranger joins
two others and thus one is reminded that the Christian liturgy begins when at least two persons are present: "Where

---

[1] Luke 24:13, 15, 17, 19-21, 27, 28-33, 35; See Luke 24:13-35 (LM, ELW,
RCL: EastEve ABC; East 3A).

[2] *Ordo Missae* or the Order of the Mass as found in *The Roman Missal*,
English Translation According to the Third Typical Edition (Collegeville:
Liturgical Press, 2011), hereafter RM.

[3] The Roman Missal refers to this fourfold pattern as Introductory Rites,
Liturgy of the Word, Liturgy of the Eucharist, and Concluding Rite.

two or three are *gathered* in my name, I am there among them" (Matt 18:20). While one may pray alone, Christian worship is always and profoundly communal, an action that draws one into relationship with others. He joins them on the first day of the week, on Sunday—not on the seventh day, the sacred day of the Sabbath set aside for worship and rest; he joins them, gathers with them, on a workday, in ordinary time as it were. These two followers, notes Luke, were saddened if not despondent: the One in whom they had placed their hope had been crucified, an ancient form of capital punishment. For them, the death of Jesus at the hands of the Roman army had seemingly closed off all contact with him. In their experience, he was moving away from them in time, never to be seen or heard again. Death had shut off all contact with him. This is the experience that accompanied them on their walk to a village.

The stranger, still unrecognized by these disciples, asks them what they are discussing. On this Sunday, they speak a story of failure and lost hope. They identify Jesus as a prophet, "mighty in deed and word," who they hoped would redeem Israel. In response, the stranger narrates and interprets Scripture—*interprets the Scriptures*—in such a way that they are enlightened. His interpretation of the ancient text responds to their need: "Were not our hearts burning within us while he was talking to us on the road, while he was opening the scriptures to us?" (Luke 24:32). Luke offers no hint of that interpretation's content and yet from their response—"our hearts were burning within us"—it was revelatory, pointing to the One they assumed had been silenced by death.

In the cultures of the ancient Mediterranean, a spontaneous invitation to *table fellowship* was nothing out of the ordinary, but the recipient was expected to decline until repeated urgings persuaded one to accept. Indeed, the sharing of food and drink at table among strangers presumed that a social bond had been established among the participants.[4] At table, then, their companion takes bread, blesses, breaks it, and gives it to them. He follows ordinary Jewish table practice and holds bread in his hands as he blesses God: "Blessed are you, LORD our God, King of the universe, you who have brought bread forth from the earth."[5] Did the companion say these words? Luke gives no indication and yet the practice of blessing God over bread and cup followed a standard pattern captured by this ancient prayer. For a loaf of bread to be shared, then, it must be broken, pulled apart, so that from the one bread the many might eat. It is in this moment and with this action that "their eyes were opened, and they recognized him." Their hearts had glowed as the risen Christ opened to them the meaning of the Scriptures but, notes Luke, they recognized him—*recognized him*—in the ordinary and domestic action of taking, blessing, breaking, and offering bread to table companions.

He vanishes from their sight. To the now enlightened disciples, a number of options present themselves. They could stay at table, complete the meal, and grapple with this unexpected and unimagined encounter. They could travel beyond Emmaus and distance themselves from Jerusalem, that place marked by death and the fear that attended those who were his followers: fear that they, too, would be arrested. After all, the men had rejected as an idle tale the women's message of his resurrection. But, instead, *they get up and go* to Jerusalem. They enter that place of seeming betrayal and loss with the news of resurrection. Their initial sadness, their disappointed hope, is transformed by this

---

[4] Bruce J. Malina and Richard L. Rohrbaugh, *Social Science Commentary on the Synoptic Gospels*, 2nd ed. (Minneapolis: Fortress Press, 2003), 323.

[5] Lucien Deiss, *Springtime of the Liturgy: Liturgical Texts of the First Four Centuries*, trans. Matthew J. O'Connell (Collegeville: Liturgical Press, 1979), 6. The dating of the text cannot be secured in the first century CE.

encounter with Christ in the Scriptures and at table—a transformation that empowers them to enter the world with surprising good news.

At first glance, this lengthy resurrection narrative appears to be the recollection of an event in the past. After all, Luke begins his gospel by informing Theophilus, his reader, that after investigating "everything," including the many "orderly accounts of the events that have been fulfilled among us," he decided to write his own account so that his reader might know the truth (Luke 1:1-4). Indeed, we know that Luke was able to draw on the Gospel of Mark, a collection of Jesus's sayings known as Q, and a collection of stories unique to this gospel, a collection not found in Mark, Matthew, or John.[6] And, yet, while Luke draws upon oral and written sources as he fashions his gospel, he is not interested in simply writing a biography of Jesus, a historical timeline filled with insightful anecdotes and sayings. Rather, he offers his readers a proclamation and an interpretation of the significance of Jesus of Nazareth, "a Savior, who is the Messiah, the Lord" (Luke 2:11).[7] Rather than a mere narrative of past events, Luke's intention in writing his gospel actually complements that of the risen Christ when he interprets the Scriptures for the two he meets on the road: as the risen Lord demonstrated how the ancient Hebrew texts hold meaning for despairing disciples in the present, so Luke presents the significance, the many meanings of Jesus, "mighty in word and deed," for his contemporary listeners, for those who

---

[6] Q from the German *Quelle*, for "source," and what some scholars refer to as Special L or the L Source, that collection of material unique to Luke. See Raymond Brown, *An Introduction to the New Testament* (New York: Doubleday, 1997), 262–267; Mark Allan Powell, *Fortress Introduction to the Gospels* (Minneapolis: Fortress Press, 1998), 15–23.

[7] Brown, *Introduction*, 227.

lived in the Roman Empire during the last third of the first century, some forty or fifty years after Jesus.[8]

Luke responds to the question of how that life then (Jesus's life, ministry, death, and resurrection) shapes and empowers Christian faith and life in the present. Thus, we find in Luke not only historical memory but also invitations, instructions, and questions for those who would hear his gospel read in the midst of the liturgical assemblies scattered throughout the ancient Mediterranean world: *instructions* as to where they would encounter the crucified and risen Lord; *invitations* to expand their understanding and practice of Christian faith and life; and *questions* to prod and stretch the imagination with the paradoxical news of a crucified Savior: How could that be? How could a Jewish peasant and preacher, crucified by Rome, be the Savior of the world?

To the question asked by late first-century Christians— "Where will we encounter the risen Christ, we who live some fifty years after 'he was carried into heaven'?"—Luke offered this instruction: you will encounter him when two or three or more of you are *gathered* for the *reading* and *interpretation* of Scripture, for *thanksgiving* and *communion* in his body broken and blood poured out, and in that world to which you are *sent*. While Luke narrates an encounter, a discussion, and a meal on a Sunday, he is, at the same time, inviting those who hear this story to recognize the presence of the risen Christ in one another (the gathering), the proclamation of the Word of God, their communion in the eucharistic gifts, and their sending into a world marked by much need. Indeed, the history of Christian worship and

---

[8] See Louis-Marie Chauvet, *Symbol and Sacrament: A Sacramental Reinterpretation of Christian Existence,* trans. Patrick Madigan and Madeleine Beaumont (Collegeville: Liturgical Press, 1995), in particular his discussion in 161–179 of Luke 24 as revelatory of the movement from nonfaith to faith.

Christian life manifests the ways in which diverse cultures in different historical epochs have embodied the pattern: some with rich elaboration (the Divine Liturgy of St. John Chrysostom) and some with noble simplicity (the Mass of the Roman Rite). And yet we recognize not only a resilient pattern that has endured for two thousand years, a living gift as it were from the first Christians, but also significant moments in that pattern.

An Exhortation to Splendid Things

One of the earliest commentators on the emerging pattern of Christian liturgy was Justin of Rome, a Hellenistic convert to Christianity, a self-styled Christian "philosopher" who suffered martyrdom during the reign of the Roman Emperor Antoninus Pius some seventy years after Luke completed his gospel. In 150, he wrote an apology or explanation of the Christian faith addressed to the emperor and his son, Marcus Aurelius.[9] In that defense of Christian faith and life, Justin narrated a second-century Roman enculturation of the Lucan pattern:

> On the day named after the sun, all who live in city or countryside assemble. The memoirs of the apostles [and] the writings of the prophets are read for as long as time allows. When the lector has finished, the president addresses us and exhorts us to imitate the splendid things we have heard. Then we all stand up and pray.
>
> When we have finished praying, bread, wine, and water are brought up. The president then prays and gives thanks according to his ability, and the people give their assent with an "Amen!" Next, the gifts over which the thanksgiving has been

---

[9] Deiss, *Springtime*, 93–94; for the critical edition see *Apologie pour les chrétiens*, vol. 507 in *Sources chrétiennes*, Intro., critical text, trans., and notes by Charles Munier (Paris: Éditions du Cerf, 2006).

spoken are distributed, and everyone shares in them, while they are also sent with the deacons to the absent brothers [and sisters]. The wealthy who are willing make contributions, each as he pleases, and the collection is deposited with the president, who aids orphans and widows, those who are in want because of sickness or some other reason, those in prison, and visiting strangers—in short, he takes care of all in need.

It is on Sunday that we all assemble, because Sunday is the first day: the day on which God transformed darkness and matter and created the world, and the day on which Jesus Christ our Savior rose from the dead . . . he appeared to his apostles and disciples and taught them what we have now offered for your examination.[10]

Whereas Luke's narrative sets forth an encounter between the risen Christ and two disciples on a road in Palestine, Justin describes a more substantial flowering of that pattern within a small Christian community located somewhere in the city of Rome.[11] Since Sunday was a workday, Christians would need to gather in the early hours of morning, most likely in a room attached to a house or in an apartment. There is a proclamation of readings by a lector from "the prophets" (the Hebrew Scriptures) and "the apostles" (the emerging Christian Scriptures). The leader is called a president, that is, the one who presides by giving an "address," giving "thanks" at table, and giving "aid" to all in need. A deacon extends the table's hospitality by bringing a portion of the bread and wine to those who are absent. A collection is taken among those who are able to give and deposited with the president, who is a guardian for all those

---

[10] *1 Apology* 67.

[11] For the possible location of the small Christian house church assemblies in Rome during the second century, see Peter Lampe, *From Paul to Valentinus: Christians at Rome in the First Two Centuries* (Minneapolis: Fortress Press, 2003), 17–47.

in need, a second extension of hospitality into the larger world beyond the liturgy.

Let us note, then, that reading from Scripture leads to an exhortation to "imitate the splendid things we have heard." That is, the president offers an interpretation of the Scriptures for a liturgical assembly living in a different culture and removed in time from the Palestinian context in which the writings of the prophets and the apostles first emerged. What meaning, what good news, can be found in an ancient Hebrew text for Gentile "Christ followers"? What good news can be heard in the writings of the apostles for an assembly of Christians who refuse to worship a deified emperor or the gods of the state? These are some of the questions Justin's preacher faced. The proclamation of Scripture thus seeks, needs, even demands interpretation if it is to become "good news" for an assembly. Such good news is not necessarily self-evident. There is thanksgiving over bread and wine (cut with water?) following the Jewish pattern of blessing God. Yet, the ancient blessing has now become a "eucharist," a thanksgiving, "glorifying the Father of the universe through the name of the Son and of the Holy Spirit."[12] Justin writes that "just as Jesus Christ our Savior was made of flesh through the word of God and took on flesh and blood for our salvation, so too through the word of prayer that comes from him, the food over which the eucharist has been spoken becomes the flesh and blood of the incarnate Jesus, in order to nourish and transform our flesh and blood."[13] Thanksgiving is made in order that, after giving their assent, the people might eat and drink, the gifts "nourishing and transforming" their flesh and blood, that is, their lives, their way of perceiving and living in this world. Yet, the liturgy does not end with the Communion.

---

[12] *1 Apology* 65.
[13] *1 Apology* 66.

While the deacons take the eucharistic food to those who are absent, the president receives a collection so that he might care for all in need: the assembly will disperse it but its dispersal is suffused with generosity. That is, the liturgy simply does not end: it continues into the larger world among those who are most vulnerable in a society in which little if any private or public program of welfare existed.

Drawn from city and countryside, Christians assemble, assemble around the Scriptures proclaimed and then interpreted. One can thus detect a movement here, one action purposefully leading to another. Indeed, Justin narrates an ensemble of actions signaled by the word *giving*: the president gives an exhortation to these "splendid things"; the president then gives thanks over the gifts of bread and wine. The president offers or gives the assembly's gifts to all who are in need, the assembly now open to the needs outside its gathering. The reading of Scripture yields to exhortation: what will come to be called a sermon or homily. Giving thanks over bread and wine yields to sharing in them—the assembly's eating and drinking. Giving gifts to the president yields to care for the poor. In other words, this ensemble of actions, of one thing purposefully yielding to another, forms a *trajectory*, a movement from gathering around the Scriptures to gathering with the poor. While the assembly moves out into work (it is a workday after all), the liturgy continues through lives "nourished and transformed," through the giving of eucharistic gifts to the absent, through the assembly's care for the orphans and widows, the sick and imprisoned, the homeless stranger and anyone else in need.

It should not surprise us, then, that Justin ends his description of this early Roman liturgy with an explanation of why Christians gather on Sunday. On the first day, "God said, 'Let there be light,' and there was light" (Gen 1:3). On the first day, writes Justin, God transformed darkness and created the world. On the first day of the week, Jesus Christ rose from the dead (Luke 24:1-12). On this day, filled with the promise of light and life emerging from darkness and death, the Christian assembly gathers as a living sign of God's life revealed in Jesus Christ; gathers around the One who speaks, who "interprets to them the things about himself in all the scriptures" (Luke 24:27); gathers around the One who transforms their flesh and blood so that they might live as his body in the world; gathers around the One who leads them to those who are in want and need. The cosmic symbol of the life-giving sun—for without the light there is no life—has become, in Justin, a metaphor of the community and its ensemble of actions: preaching speaks of splendid things, a revelatory act of enlightenment, a shedding of light on the meaning of the ancient text for this assembly's life; giving thanks to God over bread and wine includes thanksgiving for creation, for sun and earth, for the life and light revealed in Jesus; gathering a collection draws the attention and the charity of the assembly outward—its care for those who "sit in darkness and the shadow of death" (Luke 1:79) intended to feed the hungry, strengthen the weak, and support the stranger.

Rather than experiencing the liturgy as a list of rubrics or a series of things to do for a "valid" celebration, Justin describes an ensemble of actions, one leading to the other, in which the worshiping assembly encounters the presence of the risen Christ mediated through word and action. The people gather but not simply to be together, as if "community" or "hospitality" were its ultimate end or purpose. Rather, the people gather in order to hear and respond to the Word of God proclaimed, sung, interpreted, and prayed. And yet, that proclamation and interpretation yield and point to the tangible encounter with Christ in his "flesh and blood," through the earthy gifts of bread and wine: the proclamation and interpretation of Scripture—"Were not our hearts burning within us?"—point toward the Word of God coming to the assembly as food and drink—"they recognized him in the breaking of the bread." And yet—and yet—that profoundly communal and personal reception of "the flesh and blood of the incarnate Jesus" is not an end itself. The movement, the trajectory, of the liturgy draws those who receive the body and blood toward all those who are in want and need. Nourishment in "flesh and blood" is not only the reception of Christ's self-giving to others but also one's commitment to serve the flesh and blood of those in want and need.[14] Justin's ancient Roman assembly gives their assent with an "Amen!" not only as a word of agreement with the president's thanksgiving but also as their assent to the ethical implication of the gifts received: care for the orphans and widows, the sick and imprisoned, and the stranger. Here one begins to recognize the inextricable bond between sacrament and service, worship and welfare, liturgy and living in the world.

Following the Ritual Flow

The contemporary and ecumenical liturgical pattern reveals this ancient sensibility. In the Roman and other Western Rites, the people stand as they sing an acclamation to welcome the proclamation of the Gospel. In many churches, candles and incense—light, fire, and smoke—surround the proclamation. Members of the assembly may trace a cross on their foreheads, lips, and heart as they silently pray: "May the words of the Gospel be in my mind, on my lips, and in my heart." Some assemblies bow as the announcement of the Gospel is spoken and as it is concluded. In some

---

[14] See an earlier work by Louis-Marie Chauvet, *Du symbolique au symbole: Essai sur les sacrements* (Paris: Éditions du Cerf, 1979), in which he notes the movement of the liturgy as: Word given and received, Word celebrated (sacramentally), and Word lived.

rites, the priest or deacon will kiss the Gospel page at the conclusion of the reading. All of these ritual elements—standing, singing, incense, candlelight, signing the body, bowing, reading or singing the Gospel, and kissing—communicate the significance of this solemn proclamation in the liturgy: "[T]hrough their acclamations the faithful acknowledge and confess that Christ is present and is speaking to them and stand as they listen to the reading; and by the mere fact of the marks of reverence that are given to the *Book of the Gospels*."[15]

The proclamation then yields to preaching, to the interpretation of the ancient text for the assembly's current need, for its hunger to hear good news. Such preaching, therefore, is not simply an "explanation" of the Scriptures, as if the preacher's purpose is to reduce the meaning of the texts in a univocal manner. Rather, preaching is intended to provoke and nurture the faith of the gathered assembly, *their trusting receptivity to the sacramental encounter with Christ in the Eucharist*: "The sacraments are sacraments of faith, and since 'faith is born of the Word and nourished by it,' the preaching of the Word is an essential part of the celebration of the sacraments."[16] The "preaching" of the risen Christ on the road to Emmaus was a revelatory interpretation of the texts that responded to the needs of two despairing disciples, a revelation that led to the breaking of the bread. The disciples' faith in God was awakened, encouraged—"Were not our hearts burning within us while he was opening the scriptures to us?" Set next to that awakening was their ability to recognize him in the breaking of the bread.

---

[15] "General Instruction of the Roman Missal" (hereafter GIRM), in *The Roman Missal* 60.

[16] "Fulfilled in Your Hearing: The Homily in the Sunday Assembly," in *The Liturgy Documents*, 3rd ed. (Chicago: Liturgy Training Publications, 1991), 347.

Within a liturgical and sacramental context, such preaching is inextricably linked to the sacramental celebration[17] and thus leads the assembly from the table of the Word of God to the table of Christ's Body.[18] "In the Eucharistic Prayer, thanks is given to God for the whole work of salvation, and the offerings become the Body and Blood of Christ."[19] In many churches, the ritual elements that attend the proclamation of the Gospel appear again at the proclamation of the thanksgiving, the eucharistic prayer: the gifts of bread and wine are surrounded by burning lights and honored with incense; there is kneeling, bowing, raising of hands, walking, opening of hands, marking the body with a cross; one not only consumes but smells the fragrance of bread and wine; there is singing and there is silence. There is nothing less than an evangelization of all the senses and all human faculties. In contrast to the Docetic and Gnostic tendencies alive in North American cultures,[20] the movement and gestures of the body and the use of all the senses testify to the mystery of the incarnation: "Just as Jesus Christ our Savior was made of flesh through the word of God and took on flesh and blood for our salvation, so too through the word of prayer that comes from him, the food over which the eucharist has been spoken becomes the flesh

---

[17] While we focus here on the Eucharist, the same can be said for those liturgical-sacramental celebrations that follow preaching: baptism, confirmation, reconciliation (confession and forgiveness), anointing of the sick, marriage, holy orders (ordination).

[18] GIRM 28.

[19] GIRM 72.

[20] *Docetic* in reference to the ancient heresy and contemporary suggestion that Jesus masqueraded as a human being but was really a disembodied spirit; *Gnostic* in reference to the ancient and contemporary claim that all created things, including the earth and the human body, were a necessary evil, a prison for the soul or spirit, until, through a form of elitist and secret knowledge (*gnosis*), one could make one's way to a purely "spiritual" and thus disembodied state.

and blood of the incarnate Jesus, in order to nourish and transform our flesh and blood." Such thanksgiving for the embodied life of Christ gives way to reception of bread and wine. Thanksgiving is made so that the people might eat and drink, might be "fed with spiritual food, in the sacrament of his Body and Blood."[21]

And yet, such communion in the life of the risen Christ is intended to draw every member of the worshiping assembly into the world. The liturgical sending is different from an announcement that it is time to vacate the building. The deacon charges the people with their mission: "Go in peace to love and serve the Lord."[22] Why the deacon? Justin noted that the deacons bring the gifts of the table to the absent brothers and sisters. In the historical development of diaconal ministry, the deacons were and are charged with supervision of the assembly's charity among the needy within and without the Christian community. The deacon's work in the liturgy embodies the movement from Gospel proclamation (spoken or sung by a deacon), to Communion (the deacon offering the cup of wine), to sending the people into their own forms of service in the world. While the sending is frequently announced by a deacon standing in front of the altar, many churches place the dismissal into service at the threshold of the space, close to the doors through which the people move into the world, as if the deacon would charge the people to serve the Lord in daily life, turn,

---

[21] *The Book of Common Prayer* (hereafter BCP; New York: Church Publishing, 1979), 365.

[22] GIRM notes that the deacon (or the priest) sings or says the dismissal. This practice is followed in the American BCP, 366, and the Canadian *Book of Alternative Services* (Toronto: Anglican Book Centre, 1985), 215. While some Lutherans provide for a diaconal ministry, an assisting minister is charged with the dismissal, as noted in *Evangelical Lutheran Worship* (Minneapolis: Augsburg Fortress, 2006), 115.

and then lead them out of the church building—into a world beloved by God yet marked by often untold suffering.

The English word *ritual* springs from Indo-European *REI* and suggests a movement or flow of water.[23] Is it possible, then, to recognize the trajectory of Christian liturgy as a flowing of actions, one leading into another and yet drawing the previous ones into the future? For, indeed, the flow of Christian liturgy draws the assembly toward the One who is present in the temporal structure of mortality yet present with the promise of risen life, leading the assembly to live into risen life now. It is not for nothing that at the Easter Vigil the people are called upon to sing these words as they renew their baptismal promises: "I saw water flowing from the Temple, / from its right-hand side, alleluia; / and all to whom this water came were saved / and shall say: Alleluia, alleluia."[24] While God's life and salvation flow throughout this world, beyond human understanding and control, the Christian assembly lives into the promise of Christ: that where two or three are gathered in his name, he is in their midst, offering life and salvation in word and gesture. The assembly stands in the midst of the flowing action, not separate from it, not standing alone, but with all who yearn for this life and this salvation.

[23] See Robert Claiborne, *The Roots of English: A Reader's Handbook of Word Origins* (New York: Random House/Times Books, 1989), 204. *REI* can refer to a bank cut by a river or to a flow or run of water, as in a river run.

[24] "The Easter Vigil," in RM 236–237; see Ezekiel 47:1-2, 9.

Chapter Two

Discerning a Surplus of Meaning

Welcoming Eucharistic Richness

In his letter to the Christians at Ephesus, the first-century bishop and martyr Ignatius of Antioch encouraged his readers to consume eternal health in the breaking of the bread: "Break one loaf, which is the medicine of immortality; the antidote which wards off death yields continuous life in union with Jesus Christ."[1] A thousand years later, the Benedictine abbess Hildegard of Bingen would take up the image of eucharistic healing: "Blood that bled into a cry! The elements felt its touch and trembled, heaven heard their woe. O life-blood of the maker, scarlet music: salve our wounds!"[2]

Concerned that his congregation recognize themselves in the eucharistic elements, Augustine of Hippo offered an understanding of the Eucharist different from that of Ignatius: "You are there on the table; you are there in the chalice. You are this body with us, for we are this body. We drink of the same chalice because we live the same life."[3] Expanding

---

[1] Ignatius of Antioch, "Letter to the Ephesians," in *Early Christian Fathers*, ed. Cyril Richardson (New York: Macmillan, 1972), 93.

[2] Hildegard of Bingen, *Symphonia: A Critical Edition of the Symphonia Armonie Celestium Revelationum*, ed. Barbara Newman (Ithaca: Cornell University Press, 1988), 103.

[3] Augustine of Hippo, *Commentary on the Lord's Sermon on the Mount*, ed. Roy Deferrari (Washington, DC: Fathers of the Church, 1951), 322–323.

the circle of eucharistic concern, the German theologian Balthasar Fischer emphasized the encounter between those who share eucharistic bread and wine cup: "It cannot be a matter of indifference to us who else is invited to this wedding feast. Here you must greet your neighbor and say, as it were: 'How wonderful that you too have been invited to this holy table and that we may eat this holy food together.'"[4]

Yet holy food—bread and wine—do not appear out of thin air or from a sacristy cupboard; they are formed from earth's vineyards and grain fields. While much preaching, catechesis, and many hymn texts throughout Christian history tended to spiritualize eucharistic bread and wine by emphasizing the "invisible grace" over the "visible sign," the liturgical reforms of the twentieth century recovered the earthiness, the mundane nature of the gifts: "Blessed are you, Lord God of all creation, / for through your goodness we have received / the bread we offer you: / fruit of the earth . . ."[5] In his encyclical letter *Laudato Si'*, Pope Francis notes that the Eucharist not only unites heaven with earth but also "penetrates all creation. . . . Thus, the Eucharist is also a source of light and motivation for our concerns for the environment, directing us to be stewards of all creation."[6]

While the churches celebrate the institution of the Eucharist at the Mass of the Lord's Supper[7] and the supper's association with the death of Jesus, the feast of Corpus Christi (the Most Holy Body and Blood of Christ), instituted in 1264

---

[4] Fischer, *Signs, Words & Gestures*, 72.

[5] RM 23.

[6] Pope Francis, *Laudato Si': On Care for Our Common Home* (Rome: Libreria Editrice Vaticana, 2015), 152.

[7] The Maundy Thursday liturgy in Anglican and many Protestant communions.

by Pope Urban IV, attends solely to the eucharistic mystery. In 1265, Thomas Aquinas composed the sequence for the Mass of Corpus Christi, highlighting the eschatological dimension of the Eucharist, its orientation toward the future as well as the past: "Very bread, good Shepherd, tend us, Jesu, of your love befriend us . . . Grant us with your saints, though lowest, where the heavenly feast you show, fellow guests and heirs to be."[8] A similar focus on the future is found in John Arthur's offertory procession text: "Gather the hopes and the dreams of all; unite them with the prayers we offer. Grace our table with your presence, and give us a foretaste of the feast to come."[9]

Surrounded by wealthy elites in Charlemagne's imperial court, the early medieval theologian Alcuin of York underscored another dimension of the Mass: "Having received from your hands, Lord Christ, let us give with equally generous hands to those who are poor, breaking bread and sharing our bread with them."[10] Alcuin's intent was to encourage aristocratic communicants to care for the many who lived in dire poverty and were dependent on the charity of the nobility. The contemporary Brazilian theologian Leonardo Boff narrates the reality of hunger from the perspective of an impoverished communicant: "A woman went to the priest after Mass and said, 'Father, I went to communion without going to confession first.' 'How come, my daughter?' asked the priest. 'Father,' she replied, 'I arrived rather late after the offertory had begun. . . . For three days now I have had only water and nothing to eat. . . . When

---

[8] Sequence for the Solemnity of Corpus Christi, LM 266.

[9] *Lutheran Book of Worship* (Minneapolis and Philadelphia: Augsburg and LCA Board of Publication, 1978), 66.

[10] Alcuin of York, in *The HarperCollins Book of Prayers: A Treasury of Prayers throughout the Ages*, ed. Robert Van de Weyer (New York: HarperCollins, 1993), 22.

I saw you handing out the hosts, those little pieces of white bread, I went to communion just out of hunger for that little bit of bread.' "[11]

On the evening of March 24, 1980, as he stood at the altar preparing to receive bread and wine in a hospital chapel, Óscar Romero, archbishop of San Salvador, was shot dead by an assassin. Romero's commitment to the poor of El Salvador and his criticism of the government's sponsorship of terror and murder against its own people brought him into conflict not only with political leaders but also with the ruling families who controlled the country's economy. In reflection on the Eucharist, he recognized another dimension of its mystery, one that he himself would tragically experience: "This body broken and this blood shed for human beings encourage us to give our body and blood up to suffering and pain, as Christ did—not for self, but to bring justice and peace to our people."[12]

It should come as no surprise that different forms of Christianity emphasize one aspect of the eucharistic mystery over others. Among Catholics, the biblical image of sacrifice has predominated for hundreds of years: "[In the Eucharist,] the Church . . . offers the unblemished sacrificial Victim in the Holy Spirit to the Father."[13] While speaking of sacrifice as an act of thanksgiving, Anglicans have tended to emphasize memory and unity: "The Holy Eucharist is the sacrament commanded by Christ for the continual remembrance of his life, death, and resurrection . . . for the strengthening of our union with Christ."[14] While Catholics

---

[11] Leonardo Boff and Clodovis Boff, *Introducing Liberation Theology* (Maryknoll: Orbis, 1987), 1.

[12] Óscar Romero, *A Martyr's Message of Hope: Six Homilies by Archbishop Óscar Romero* (Kansas City: Celebration Books, 1981), 166.

[13] GIRM 79.

[14] "The Catechism," in *The Book of Common Prayer* 1979, 859–860.

and Anglicans consider the Eucharist one means through which God offers the remission of sin, Lutherans, following Martin Luther's lead, have given particular attention to this dimension of the Eucharist: "The words 'given for you' and 'shed for you for the forgiveness of sin' show us that forgiveness of sin, life, and salvation are given to us in the sacrament through these words, because where there is forgiveness of sin, there is also life and salvation."[15]

Such a description of denominational emphases is not to suggest that other dimensions of eucharistic meaning are absent in these three forms of Christianity. Rather, it is to suggest that a particular emphasis runs the risk of marginalizing other significant meanings in light of two millennia of Christian reflection: the medicine of immortality; salve for wounds; nourishment for the baptized; food and drink shared with neighbors; gifts of the earth; stewardship of creation; a foretaste of the feast to come; bread for the poor; food for a hungry woman; and sustenance for the work of justice and peace. The storehouse of Christian tradition reveals a rich treasure of eucharistic images, a diverse array that stands in stark contrast to the fundamentalist preference for one unchanging viewpoint. Forgoing subscription to a single perspective, the many hymns, sequences, liturgical texts, artwork, sermons, prayers, mystical writings, and commentaries of the Christian tradition stretch the imagination to think beyond the known and familiar. Indeed, such expansive thinking can be unnerving to the timid and the insecure because it welcomes stories and images that might call into question a world painted in one single color, a way of thinking circumscribed by closed

---

[15] Martin Luther, "Small Catechism," in *The Book of Concord: The Confessions of the Evangelical Lutheran Church*, ed. Robert Kolb and Timothy Wengert (Minneapolis: Fortress Press, 2000), 362.

boundaries. In the keeping of a closed field of meaning, there is much pastoral peril.

Symbolic Surplus

Scholars of literary theory and ritual anthropology point to *symbol* as an appropriate description of the rich imagery found in Scripture, liturgical texts, hymns, artwork, and rituals. Popular use of the term *symbol*, however, appears when an action is perceived to be devoid of meaning. For instance, a news reporter notes that "in a symbolic act, the United Nations voted to approve a measure encouraging the reduction of world hunger. Yet until nations actually change their budget priorities, the vote remains an empty act." Or this: a symbol may represent something else but have no intrinsic value in itself, as in "It's only a symbol." In contrast to these conventional and widespread views, a more nuanced understanding takes its cue from the word itself: English "symbol" is derived from Greek *symbolein*, a throwing or clustering together of many things (*sun/sym*: together; *ballo*: throw). Thus, a symbol or symbolic word, act, person, or thing is capable of gathering more than one thing within itself, *holding together a range of meanings*.[16] There is versatile content in a symbolic word, act, person, or thing. No wonder Jesus is understood as symbolic person: Mark portrays him as a suffering martyr; Matthew presents him as teacher and reviser of Torah; Luke highlights his public ministry as prophet and liberator; John sees him as

[16] The literature on the symbolic nature of biblical and liturgical language is extensive. Consider the following: F. W. Dillistone, *Traditional Symbols and the Contemporary World* (London: Epworth, 1973), 10–28; Thomas Fawcett, *The Symbolic Language of Religion* (Minneapolis: Augsburg, 1971), 26–38; Gail Ramshaw, *Liturgical Language: Keeping It Metaphoric, Making It Inclusive* (Collegeville: Liturgical Press, 1996), 25–34; Paul Ricoeur, *The Symbolism of Evil* (Boston: Beacon, 1986), 10–14.

the creating Word of God made flesh in human history. Do not all of these diverse images speak the truth of who he is? Yet, not one of them exhausts the surplus of meaning that has been discovered in him over two thousand years.

In contrast to the univocal nature of "sign" (for example, a red sign means only one thing: Stop), a symbol is multivocal, capable of more than one "voice." As a word, action, person, or thing that welcomes more than one meaning, symbol is polyvalent, many-valued; it is resistant to reduction—even though some may be quite satisfied with the safety of one voice, one meaning. Just as it has canonized diverse portrayals of the one Jesus, the Christian tradition reveals different dimensions of the one eucharistic practice. Indeed, it would seem that one interpretation is not sufficient to capture or pin down "the inexhaustible richness of this sacrament."[17] The language of sign values exactitude and rightfully closes meaning: anyone sitting in an emergency room wants to know that the nurse and attending physician grasp the difference between a gram and a milligram; ambiguity spells potential disaster when precision is the one thing needed. But the language of religion and, thus, the language of sacramental Christianity, is the language of metaphor and ritual in which symbol opens up and expands. For the precision minded, symbol can appear messy and chaotic. Indeed, opening up and expanding the images that cluster around the Eucharist can, for some, be annoying if not threatening. What if the Eucharist were about more than Christ's *sacrifice*, more than the *remembrance* of his saving life, more than the *forgiveness* of sins or God's mercy?

Consider the various images that expand the meaning of this ritual practice. It is the *Breaking of the Bread*, for all who eat of the broken bread participate in Christian faith and

---

[17] *The Catechism of the Catholic Church*, 2nd ed. (Rome: Libreria Editrice Vaticana, 1997/2000), 335.

life, this shared participation is a challenge to the robust individualism of the West.[18] St. Paul speaks of the *Lord's Supper*, for it is Christ who is the host, a helpful antidote to any attempt by clergy to assume control over what is the Lord's command to "do this in memory of me."[19] The supper is commonly called *Eucharist*, an act of thanksgiving to God for creation and the new creation wrought in Christ's passing over from death to life, his resurrection a rising into his water-washed and anointed Body.[20] The supper is also a *Holy Communion*, for through the gifts of bread and wine Christ unites himself intimately to each seeking soul and draws each one into relationship with him. St. Paul asks the Christians at Corinth, "The cup of blessing that we bless, is it not a communion in the blood of Christ? The bread that we break, is it not a communion in the body of Christ?"[21] Among Eastern Catholics and Orthodox communions, the

[18] Matthew 5:36; 14:19.

[19] 1 Corinthians 11:20. Let us be clear: the Eucharist needs well-trained and thoughtful leadership in order to avoid a "mechanistic" understanding of the Eucharist (that is, the notion that one only needs the designated minister to say the "right words"—either the words of the Roman Missal or the biblical institution narrative found in many Protestant worship books, a view, I might add, subject to magical thinking). What is criticized here is the tendency among some to forget that the presider or celebrant is not the host and thus not the center of attention and thus not the one who "controls" the Eucharist. Rather, the presider or celebrant serves the One who is the host and thus this service ought to be grounded in a robust theology of the Eucharist and a transparent manner of presiding that serves the central symbols rather than obscures them or simply highlights the personality of the presider. See Robert Hovda, *Strong, Loving and Wise: Presiding in Liturgy*, 5th ed. (Collegeville: Liturgical Press, 1981); Aidan Kavanagh, *Elements of Rite: A Handbook of Liturgical Style* (Collegeville: Liturgical Press, 1990); Patrick Malloy, *Celebrating the Eucharist: A Practical Ceremonial Guide for Clergy and Other Liturgical Ministers* (New York: Church Publishing, 2007).

[20] Luke 22:19.

[21] 1 Corinthians 10:16.

Divine Liturgy welcomes worshipers into the heavenly liturgy that transcends time and space, a liturgy that highlights the company of martyrs, saints, and angels, thus pointing the assembly to a great cloud of witnesses who join them in worship and assist them with their prayers. The Latin dismissal from the liturgy—*Ite, missa est*—sends the assembly forth to embody the words and actions of the *Mass*, the *missa*. In contrast to the Orthodox emphasis on entering into the heavenly liturgy, the Roman and thus Western trajectory of the liturgy stresses engagement in this world.[22]

This diversity of eucharistic images is also present in the lyrics sung by the assembly.[23]

---

[22] This is not to suggest that Eastern Catholic and Orthodox communions are not concerned with life in this world or that Western Christians know nothing of the eschatological dimension of the Eucharist. Here we simply indicate strong emphases that do not rule out other ones.

[23] This, however, is a not a universal practice. Some collections, Catholic and Protestant, present flat, unimaginative paraphrases of biblical texts (one wonders: Why not use the original text itself?) or variations on one theme (for example, "We are the body of Christ," or "We are nourished on bread and wine"). The point is this: the six images discussed above in Anglican, Catholic, and Protestant catechetical sources—a very *basic* and limited set of images at that—are not reflected in a number of collections. By way of contrast, in those collections that offer a global and historical representation of eucharistic hymns, there appears a more diverse array of images. One might also consider the highly questionable practice of the assembly singing as if it were the God of Israel or Jesus Christ ("Eat this bread, drink this cup, come to me and never be hungry," "I am the Bread of life, you who come to me shall not hunger," "I will come to you in the silence," "I, the Lord of sea and sky"). While this wording has appeared in recently composed and "contemporary" Catholic collections (and incorporated into some Protestant hymnals), one has to wonder if hymn writers and publishers were aware that the Eucharist is a *dialogical* ritual in which the assembly addresses the Holy Three and the voice of the Holy Three is heard in the proclamation of the Word of God throughout the liturgy. The assembly is not the Second Person of the Holy Trinity or the God of Israel singing to him or herself.

"Let us break bread together on our knees; let us break bread together on our knees; when I fall on my knees, with my face to the rising sun, O Lord, have mercy on me."[24]

"As the fields of wheat now growing will become a holy sign, so shall we reveal you, Jesus, that in us you now may shine. Like the grape put in the cellar, there to change into the wine, all the poor on earth who suffer shed their sorrows in this sign."[25]

"Father, we thank you who has planted your holy Name within our hearts. Knowledge and faith and life immortal Jesus your Son to us imparts. Lord, you did make all for your pleasure, did give us food for all our days, giving in Christ the Bread eternal; yours is the pow'r, be yours the praise."[26]

"O bread of life from heaven, O food to pilgrims given, O manna from above: feed with the blessed sweetness of your divine completeness the souls that want and need your love."[27]

The assembly does not give the Eucharist to itself but receives it from Christ; note the pre-Communion invitations and confession: "The Gifts of God for the People of God" (BCP 364); "Taste and see that the Lord is good" (ELW 112); "Lord, I am not worthy that you should enter under my roof" (RM 521). One wonders: Have the Psalms—the preeminent tutor in public Christian praying and its dialogical nature—simply disappeared?

[24] American folk hymn in *Gather Comprehensive* (Chicago: GIA Publications, 1994), 832.

[25] Jose de la Jara Alonso, from "Misa Popular Campesina de Nicaragua," in *La Gaceta* 234 (October 1971); author's trans.

[26] From "The Didache" (2nd c.), trans. Bland Tucker, in *Hymnal 1982* (New York: Church Publishing, 1985), 302.

[27] Thomas Aquinas, "O Esca viatorum" (c. 1661), trans. Hugh T. Henry, in *The American Catholic Hymnal* (New York: P.J. Kennedy & Sons, 1913), 320.

"At the Lamb's high feast we sing praise to our victorious King, who has washed us in the tide flowing from his piercéd side; praise we him, whose love divine gives his sacred Blood for wine, gives his Body for the feast, Christ the victim, Christ the priest."[28]

The images tumble over each other: breaking bread while facing the east from whence the light of Christ appears; poor laborers shedding their sorrows in the supper's wine; thanksgiving for the seed planting that gives life; a gathering becoming a communion of friends; manna falling from above to nourish the soul; the heavenly liturgy—the Lamb's feast—alive in the earthly liturgy. Each text, and the many others not mentioned here, manifest particular situations that have prompted Christians and Christian lyricists to recognize a dimension of the eucharistic mystery that responds to their need, their hope, perhaps their tragedy. Indeed, it is in the juxtaposition of the Eucharist with human experience that fresh insight is gained on its inexhaustible richness.

The Pastoral Significance of Symbolic Richness

Yet, one might rightly wonder if any discussion of symbolic richness is simply an exercise in literary antiquarianism. After all, the pragmatic soul of the West is drawn toward fixing things, growing things, achieving something, making a difference and being remembered for it.[29] What

---

[28] Hymn in the Ambrosian tradition, trans. Robert Campbell, in *Gather Comprehensive*, 433.

[29] While the language of Greece has been tied to aesthetic and philosophical interests, to the divinization of the Christian, the language of Rome and its legacy in North America have shaped the practical arts: law and public works, and social morality, all eminently "useful" concerns.

good is there in contemplating different literary designa-
tions of a ritual that in most places consumes less than an
hour each week? But, then, on second thought, might the
larger field of meaning discovered in this primary and public act respond to particular needs—the human experience—
alive in the assembly, in the community of faith?

Consider, for instance, the "utilitarian individual" who
seems to have triumphed in North American life.[30] This is
the personality shaped by a society that values the individual over community, the personality that wants to go it
alone in the world. Oh, he or she may be married and have
children but the deep motivator in life is the need to be free
and floating, taking what he or she can and then moving
on, not being pinned down.[31] North American cities—where
most citizens now live—draw newcomers with the promise
of anonymity, a contrast to life in small towns and rural
villages. And yet there is a steep price to pay for seeking
anonymity and "doing it my way," and that is the disorient-
ing experience of loneliness, of having no significant and
meaningful attachments, of being "at the top" professionally
but all alone at the top. Is that not a terrible burden to bear,
in truth a denial of one's social nature?

One of the deepest suspicions of organized religion and
its rituals is that they promote conformity to rules and regu-
lations and smother any sense of personal agency. But is
such a suspicion celebrated in the Eucharist? Rather, does
the Eucharist not hold forth the possibility of attachment to
other people, of *breaking bread with friends*, and having one's
God-given dignity and distinctive gifts honored? Might the
image of sharing bread with companions respond to the

---

[30] Robert Bellah, Richard Madsen, William Sullivan, Ann Swidler, and
Steve Tipton, *Habits of the Heart: Individualism and Commitment in American
Life* (Berkeley: University of California Press, 1985/1996), 27–52.

[31] One wonders if there is any connection between this personality and
the soaring rate of divorce in "traditional" marriages.

one who is adrift in loneliness? "The bread is broken and the wine poured out so that all of us 'separate' persons can share and become one like the loaf and cup that were previously whole. [And] this sharing welcomes both freedom and fulfillment for the person and the person's love and unity and peace and communion with others."[32]

Or consider this: the temptation may be present among pastoral leaders to assume that people gather for the Eucharist because they enjoy the community, the beauty of the music, programs for children, or pastoral care from birth to death. Maybe they return week after week because the preaching is comforting in a world that seems to offer little consolation. What of those, however, who yearn for neither the music nor children's program but this one thing: to be drawn into the mystery of God? What of those who have fallen in love with the "bridegroom of the soul" and seek greater union with him? Are they viewed with benign skepticism as if they had stepped out of a medieval convent into a world that views such yearnings as neuroses best cured in therapy? It is quite ironic that in a culture focused so intently on the intimacy of the bedroom, the desire for an intimate union with the divine can be viewed as odd. But, then, what of the church: throughout its history, many ecclesial leaders have harbored suspicions that the mystic may well transcend or criticize clerical authority. Just think of the many women mystics—all of them daily communicants devoted to the Eucharist—who were pushed to profess their assumed lowliness, their assumed littleness, their "almost nothingness" in order to allay the fears of male leaders, allay their fears so that the mystic might speak the truth of God's great and equitable love for every soul. "O Wealth of the Poor," wrote Teresa of Avila, one of the most down-to-earth mystics in history, "how wonderfully can you sustain souls,

---

[32] Robert Hovda, *It Is Your Own Mystery* (Silver Spring: The Liturgical Conference, 1977).

revealing your great riches to them. I have never seen such great Majesty hidden in a thing so small as a Host without marveling at your great wisdom."[33] Or this, from the Lutheran hymn writer Johannes Franck: "Soul, adorn yourself with gladness, leave the gloomy haunts of sadness, come into the daylight's splendor, there with joy your praises render. Bless the One whose grace unbounded this amazing banquet founded; Christ, though heav'nly, high, and holy, deigns to dwell with you most lowly. Hasten as a bride to meet him, eagerly and gladly greet him."[34]

It should come as no surprise that the Holy Communion points to a relationship. And it should surprise no one— Anglican, Catholic, or Protestant—that the term *communion* speaks of an intimacy deeper than receiving the forgiveness of one's sin. The reception of bread and wine can be understood, and at times reductively, as food and drink for the people of God, as the visible sign of a significant event in the past, or as the means through which "grace" is bestowed upon the communicant. Yet, is it not appropriate to move from a reductive to an expansive understanding of the Holy Communion, one in which the seeking soul encounters the living presence of a person—of Christ the Lover—who desires relationship and gives himself freely to the seeking soul? "Come and leave your loved one never; dwell within my heart forever."[35]

Beyond Me and Us

What of those who weary of religion as nothing more than comforting talk for the socially comfortable? While it

---

[33] Teresa of Avila, *Selected Writings of St. Teresa of Avila*, ed. William Doheny (Milwaukee: Bruce Publishing, 1950), 57.

[34] Johannes Franck, "Soul, Adorn Yourself with Gladness," in *ELW*, 488.

[35] Franck, "Soul, Adorn Yourself with Gladness."

may not be difficult to proclaim the love of Christ for the individual and for the Christian community, the thoughtful person will ask: What next? How does that "love" take shape in daily life? What, then, of the worshiper who is well aware of the gross injustices that mark human life? Is such a concern alien to the celebration of the Eucharist? Indeed, too often one encounters a dichotomy between faith in the sacrament and the faith that seeks justice. If one's understanding of the Eucharist resides solely in the metaphor of communion, of the Mass as community-building ritual or personal union with Christ or "God-centered worship," such a singular focus needs to be placed next to the prophetic mission of Jesus, a mission embedded in this eucharistic prayer: "To the poor he proclaimed the good news of salvation, / to prisoners, freedom, / and to the sorrowful of heart, joy."[36] Does this text not open up the meaning of the Eucharist and the relationship between the *Mass*—being sent out—and the passion of Christ for those who live with the burden of poverty, oppression, and injustice? After all, the ancient dismissal, *Ite*, is not a polite invitation to linger at the church's door. It is a command, voiced in the imperative, and addressed to the whole assembly: You all go now! You all leave! That is, you go forth to bring good news to the poor, release to captives, and freedom for the oppressed.

Consider, again, Óscar Romero, who was murdered at the altar because he insisted that the suffering of Christ— revealed in eucharistic Body and Blood—nourished the work of justice and peace among the many poor of El Salvador,

---

[36] RM 117; BCP 375—inspired by Jesus claiming the mission of the prophet: "The Spirit of the Lord is upon me, because he has anointed me to bring good news to the poor. He has sent me to proclaim release to the captives and recovery of sight to the blind, to let the oppressed go free, to proclaim the year of the Lord's favor" (Luke 4:18-19). For a similar theme, see Thanksgiving VIII in ELW, 67: "You sent your chosen servant to preach good news to the afflicted, to break bread with the outcast and despised."

a work that led him to criticize the corrupt government of his nation whose political leaders could be found at Mass every Sunday. If he had preached the Eucharist as one thing and one thing only—the spiritual love of God for the soul— rather than the call to act with justice in a society marked by violent injustice, he may well have escaped the threats made on his life. One wonders what he recognized in the Eucharist that others failed to see.

Or this: if wine is the "fruit of the vine and work of human hands" that becomes "our spiritual drink,"[37] would the use of wine in the Eucharist not lead one to consider its place of origin? Such reflection might then lead one to consider the plight of laborers in American vineyards, many who live in desperately poor conditions and earn less than a living wage. Would it be ironic, if not hypocritical, to receive wine, the Blood of Christ, created in conditions of social injustice? Not only is the wine "our spiritual drink," the drink is also imprinted with the conditions of its creation.

Or this: while one may rest in prayerful adoration before the Blessed Sacrament—the icon and embodiment of Christ's passion—does such prayer include the suffering of the poor and draw one into the work of promoting economic justice? It would seem that the "inexhaustible richness of the sacrament" militates against the human tendency to rest comfortably with one image alone.[38]

What did Teresa of Calcutta say? "In the Mass we have Jesus in the broken bread and in the slums we touch him in

---

[37] RM 15.

[38] Consider as well the different aspects of the Mass as enumerated in *A Eucharist Sourcebook,* ed. Robert Baker and Barbara Budde (Chicago: Liturgy Training Publications, 1999): Hungering, Gathering, Praying, Remembering, Offering, Eating and Drinking, Healing, Feeding the World, and Corpus Christi.

broken bodies and abandoned children."[39] Does the Eucharist not hold these two together in uneasy juxtaposition: broken bread and broken bodies? And in that juxtaposition, absent any moralizing, can one not discern the *missio* of Jesus and his friends? For the claim made here is that the eucharistic images alive in the Christian community draw one not only into a personal encounter with the sacramental Christ, not only into a communion with others gathered around the altar, but, rather, the Mass, the Holy Communion, orients the assembly outward to the world, to a world marked by unholy violence and injustice. "What one witnesses in the liturgy is the world being done as the world's Creator and Redeemer will the world to be done. The liturgy does the world and does it at its very center, for it is here that the world's malaise and its cure well up together, inextricably entwined."[40]

[39] Malcolm Muggeridge, *Something Beautiful for God: Mother Teresa of Calcutta* (New York: Harper & Row, 1971), 92.

[40] Kavanagh, *Elements of Rite*, 44.

Chapter Three

Eating with the Hungry
and the Outcast

Invitations and Admonitions

While the medieval Lectionary presented only two readings for every Sunday and feast day, a cycle that was unchanging from year to year, the three-year lectionary of the
late twentieth century has expanded not only the number
of readings for each Sunday and feast day but also revealed
a richness of images that cluster around and interpret the
meal practice of Jesus and his first followers who lived in
the ancient Mediterranean world. If we discern differing
theological portraits of Jesus in the New Testament, would
we not also expect to find a large field of food, meal, or
banquet metaphors? Christian communions may well
cherish a particular understanding of the Eucharist (such
as "sacrifice," "remembrance," "forgiveness"), yet the New
Testament invites one to engage in a more nuanced discernment of texts that contribute to the symbolic richness of this
primary sacrament. Thus, it is important to recognize that
as the reformed Lectionary of Vatican II was promulgated
and other lectionaries were developed in its light, biblical
and liturgical scholars were examining the relationship between the many meal texts in the Bible and their potential
relationship to the church's Eucharist.

Scripture scholars invite Christian communities to study and interpret the gospels, to read and hear them *not* as simple biographical portraits of Jesus and his disciples (no New Testament writer was an eyewitness to the historical Jesus), but as carefully constructed proclamations of the good news: Gospel proclamations that hold *historical memories* (passed on in oral and written traditions) interwoven with *instructions* and *invitations* to the Christian communities addressed by the gospel writers, communities that began to emerge after 30 CE in various regions of the Mediterranean. While the gospels offer good news regarding the person and mission of Jesus, they also reveal the questions, struggles, and conflicts alive in the communities for whom the writers fashioned their gospels. For instance, Mark wrote in the 60s to Christ followers who were wondering if they would be persecuted by the Roman imperial army in the midst of the Jewish Revolt (66–70 CE). Writing some ten to twenty years after Mark, Matthew addressed a community experiencing conflict between its Jewish Christ followers and Gentile Christ followers. Luke, creating his gospel at the same time as Matthew, wrote to Gentile Christ followers throughout the Mediterranean world who knew little of the Jewishness of Jesus and thus wondered what it meant to be a Gentile follower of Jesus. And the Gospel of John, edited toward the end of the first century, addressed a community that was experiencing a tragic divorce from its matrix in rabbinic Judaism, a divorce that left them wondering how they would survive.

Though the evangelists may not say so explicitly, the house communities to which they addressed their gospels were ritual communities in which they practiced water-washing, anointing with olive oil, giving thanks to God over bread and wine, singing, reading from the Hebrew Scriptures, and listening to a gospel or letter proclaimed—but practiced within the context of their unique questions, struggles, and conflicts. Thus, the gospels as well as other New Testament texts frequently address and reflect the meal practices of these little church gatherings in the last half of the first century[1]—both in their faithfulness to Jesus's practice in the first third of the century and in their failure to live into his practice. Consider, for instance, Jesus's instruction in the Gospel of Luke:

> When you give a luncheon or a dinner, do not invite your friends or your brothers or your relatives or rich neighbors, in case they may invite you in return, and you would be repaid. But when you give a banquet, invite the poor, the crippled, the lame, and the blind. And you will be blessed, because they cannot repay you, for you will be repaid at the resurrection of the righteous.[2]

At first glance the text appears to be advice offered by Jesus to a religious leader who invited him to a Sabbath meal. But, then one needs to ask: Why did Luke include this memory of Jesus in a gospel written in the 80s to 90s and addressed to literate and well-off "God-lovers"[3] in the Roman Empire, an empire in which common meal practice knew nothing—*nothing*—of welcoming the poor and disabled to a banquet sponsored by a wealthy host? Social classes did not mix in table fellowship. Indeed, a poor person at a banquet would not be seated with the master, the *dominus*, of the household but, rather, with the slave or servant assisting in the preparations and serving of the meal.

---

[1] Here we include the letters of the historical Paul from the 50s and early 60s.

[2] Luke 14:1, 7-14 (LM: Ord 22C; ELW: L 22C; RCL: Pr. 17C).

[3] Luke addresses his gospel to Theophilus ("a lover of God"), a highly uncommon name, leading Scripture scholars to suggest that Luke wrote for a broad range of Gentiles—"God lovers"—in the ancient Mediterranean.

Is it possible that through Jesus's exhortation, Luke is giving an instruction to his audience of Gentile Christians concerning the practice of Jesus and their need to follow that practice if they are to claim that their sharing of bread, supper, and wine cup is truly in "memory of him"? In other words, is Luke suggesting to the communities reading his gospel on a Sunday morning that Jesus was found among the poor, crippled, lame, and blind? And is the advice actually a question directed to the ritual communities listening to this story: *Are the poor and the destitute among you, with you?* One wonders if the cultural power of closed or exclusive meals had begun to change Christian practice and, thus, was Luke offering his readers a forceful admonition: Why are those associated with another social class—culturally perceived as "inferior"—not present when you gather for the breaking of the bread? Such an admonition should not be a surprise: some thirty years earlier, Paul criticized wealthy Christ followers at Corinth for their disregard, their contempt, of poor Christ followers, a criticism that led Paul to conclude that they had, in fact, *not* celebrated the Lord's Supper.[4]

This is to suggest that historical memories of Jesus's sayings and actions were employed strategically by the evangelists to address the ritual practice of Christ followers, of nascent Christian communities—though not only the ritual practice. Rather than a news reporter's eyewitness account of what happened from day to day or week to week in the life of Jesus, the evangelist is drawing on memories in order to "proclaim the good news of Jesus Christ, the Son of God."[5] Part of that proclamation is the good news that Jesus viewed those who struggled with poverty and physical hardships far differently than the dominant culture in which he lived; indeed, he was known, at times scandalously

[4] 1 Corinthians 11:20-22.
[5] Mark 1:1.

known, for sharing food and drink—and thus life—with them. By including this memory of Jesus at a Sabbath meal, Luke may well be asking the Christ followers who read his gospel in the Sunday gathering if they, too, are living into this good news through the countercultural act of honoring the poor and those with physical hardships who in every other setting would be excluded from the banquet table and the breaking of bread among friends.[6]

Food for Hungry People

Could a Lucan exhortation concerning Mediterranean banquet practice be a reference to what Luke calls "the breaking of the bread," to giving thanks over bread, sharing supper, and giving thanks over the wine cup, giving thanks to God for creation and redemption—what will come to be called the Eucharist? A good number of scholars think so.[7] And if such is the case, then other meal references in the gospels and letters, as well as meal texts in the Hebrew Scriptures, may well open up one's understanding of the

---

[6] Luke uses terms to describe persons who were physically challenged and economically disenfranchised. The thoughtful catechist, teacher, intercessor, preacher, and musician will want to consider how best to speak about persons who may suffer from cultural stereotypes that equate one's personhood with a temporary or permanent condition: people who are challenged by poverty; persons who are challenged with a physical limitation.

[7] Robert Karris, *Eating Your Way Through Luke's Gospel* (Collegeville: Liturgical Press, 2006); Gordon Lathrop, *The Four Gospels on Sunday: The New Testament and the Reform of Christian Worship* (Minneapolis: Fortress Press, 2012); Eugene Laverdiere, *Dining in the Kingdom of God: The Origins of Eucharist according to Luke* (Chicago: Liturgy Training Publications, 2007); Laverdiere, *The Breaking of the Bread: The Development of the Eucharist according to Acts* (Chicago: Liturgy Training Publications, 2007); Graydon Snyder, *Inculturation of the Jesus Tradition: The Impact of Jesus on Jewish and Roman Cultures* (London: Bloomsbury T & T Clark, 1999).

Eucharist and thus enhance the "inexhaustible richness of the sacrament."[8]

Consider this catena of images. Pregnant with child, Mary announces, "[T]he Mighty One has done great things for me . . . he has filled the hungry with good things, and sent the rich away empty."[9] The adult Jesus mirrors this startling revelation when he proclaims: "Blessed are you who are hungry now, for you will be filled. . . . Woe to you who are full now, for you will be hungry."[10] When asked by a disciple, "Teach us to pray," he invites them to say: "Give us each day our daily bread,"[11] a petition offered in the

---

[8] Christians do not keep a "meal" when they celebrate the Eucharist. While some communions include a shorthand version of the *Ordo Missae* in their worship books and Sunday worship leaflets (for example, gathering, word, meal, sending), the adoption of such an outline seems to overlook its Christian character: not Word, but the Word of God; not Meal but the Liturgy of the Eucharist or the Holy Communion. The meal referred to in the Last Supper narratives dropped out of Christian sacramental practice when Emperor Trajan (53–117 CE) banned supper clubs, concerned that they could be or become centers of sedition. Christians retained the blessing of God over bread followed by the blessing of God over wine—ritual blessings inherited from Jewish practice. If anything, contemporary Christians keep a portion of an ancient Mediterranean meal in ritual form or they keep a Christianized form of a Jewish table blessing.

[9] Luke 1:49, 53; excerpted from the Song of Mary, the *Magnificat*.

[10] Luke 6:21, 25; part of the Lucan beatitudes that focus on economic and social conditions, a contrast—some say—to the Matthean beatitudes, but see Warren Carter, *Matthew and the Margins: A Sociopolitical and Religious Reading* (Maryknoll: Orbis, 2000), 128–137.

[11] Luke 11:3. This petition, which may be translated as "Give us our bread for tomorrow," has been interpreted sacramentally as the bread of the Eucharist and as an eschatological yearning for the coming of the kingdom of God. But consider also the economic context of peasant culture in first-century Roman Palestine in which physical hunger was a daily threat to life. See Douglas Oakman, "The Tables and the Table," in *The Political Aims of Jesus* (Minneapolis: Fortress Press, 2012), 79–101;

midst of peasant hunger. He tells a parable of the indifference of the rich to physical suffering: "There was a rich man who was dressed in purple and fine linen and who feasted sumptuously every day. And at his gate lay a poor man named Lazarus, covered with sores, who longed to satisfy his hunger with what fell from the rich man's table."[12] There seems to be a pointed concern in Luke's gospel for *people who experience physical hunger* and wonder anxiously if there will be sufficient bread to feed their children tomorrow. After all, in the public announcement of his mission, the Lucan Jesus identifies himself with the prophetic tradition: "The Spirit has anointed me to bring good news to the poor."[13] And who were the prophets?[14] Those who were called and consecrated by God to address the people of God, diagnose departures from the covenant—departures frequently manifested in social inequity and corruption—and then offer an alternative to the growth of social injustice, such as the failure to provide adequate food and drink for the hungry poor.

Perhaps, though, if one has never experienced chronic hunger due to the privilege of gender, race, education, and economic advantage, the stark reality of hunger in the ancient world and its persistence in the world today simply slides out of view: "Lord, when was it that we saw you

---

and Oakman, "The Lord's Prayer in Social Perspective," in *Jesus, Debt and the Lord's Prayer* (Eugene: Wipf & Stock, 2014), 42–91.

[12] For the entire parable, see Luke 16:19-31. The parable has been interpreted as a call to repentance, to conversion of life. One rightly asks: repentance or conversion of life toward what, to what end?

[13] Luke 4:18. Luke has collected a series of quotations: Isaiah 61:1; 58:6; 61:2.

[14] Consider Walter Brueggemann, *The Prophetic Imagination*, 2nd ed. (Minneapolis: Fortress Press, 2001); Marcus Borg, "Jesus as Prophet: A Social World in Crisis," in *Jesus: A New Vision* (New York: Harper Collins, 1991), 150–171.

hungry?"[15] When the debilitating force of hunger has no hold in one's consciousness, it is far too easy to interpret biblical texts in a spiritualized fashion as a "hunger" for God, for spiritual fulfillment, or for a Christian virtue. Indeed, it is not that difficult to avoid a challenging text that might call into question one's priorities or the economic system from which some benefit while many suffer. When the Eucharist is experienced solely as a personal and private encounter with Christ or as a community-cohesion practice, one can readily imagine that the Eucharist has little if anything to do with the experience of chronic hunger.[16]

And yet, it is impossible to avoid the persistence of debilitating hunger in human life and in the experience of the ancestors: "All look to you, O God, to give them their food in due season; when you give to them, they gather it up; when you open your hand, they are filled with good things."[17] "Is not this the fast that I choose . . . to share your bread with the hungry?"[18] God feeds all creatures through the agency of the natural world. God intends that God's creatures flourish on earth. God urges the people of God to share bread so that no one suffers in hunger. Is it possible that in the economy of God no one ever goes hungry because there is an equitable distribution of food and drink? Would this not be good news—gospel—for the many who suffered and suffer with food insecurity? For Luke, *salvation happens in the present* and salvation is directly related to those

---

[15] Matthew 25:36.

[16] Various offices and organizations in the United States chronicle the state of "food insecurity" (chronic hunger): the Economic Research Service of the U.S. Department of Agriculture; Catholic Charities USA; Bread for the World; Feed the Children.

[17] Psalm 104:27-28 (LM: Pent Vigil ABC, Pent ABC; ELW: Pent ABC, L 29B; RCL: Pent ABC, Pr. 24B).

[18] Isaiah 58:6-7; see Isaiah 58:7-10 (LM: Ord 5A; ELW/RCL: Epi 5A, Ash ABC).

conditions that diminish, dehumanize, and deal death. Thus, salvation may be the forgiveness of sin, but salvation can also be experienced as healing from infirmity. In Luke's gospel, "feeding the hungry is a saving act."[19] Was it this practice of an equitable sharing of food and drink to which Jesus alludes when he announces his mission to "proclaim a year of the Lord's favor"?[20] But, then, for this gracious and life-giving economy to flourish, an economy that serves the well-being of God's earth and all God's creatures, would there not need to be a reform of the present economy focused solely on the accumulation of wealth for the individual or the corporation?

The Gospel of Mark holds the earliest reference to the feeding of a great crowd in a deserted place.[21] The evangelist alludes to the feeding of the Hebrews in the wilderness through Moses (Exodus 16 and Numbers 11) as well as the feeding of Elijah in a time of famine (1 Kings 4). Set before the story of Jesus's wilderness feeding is the gruesome narration of Herod's execution of John the Baptizer, whose severed head is served on a platter at the ruler's birthday banquet. One meal scene is set in juxtaposition to another: with predatory and exploitative rulers, there is only death;

---

[19] Powell, *Fortress Introduction to the Gospels*, 106.

[20] Luke 4:19, "the year of the Lord's favor," is a reference to the biblical Jubilee as recorded in Leviticus 25:1-55; see the Apostolic Letter of St. John Paul II, *As the Third Millennium Draws Near*, in which he raises awareness of the economic implications of the Jubilee year in terms of forgiveness of debt and advocacy for the poor, at: https://w2.vatican.va/content /john-paul-ii/en/apost_letters/1994/documents/hf_jp-ii_apl_19941110 _tertio-millennio-adveniente.html; see also Richard Lowery, *Sabbath and Jubilee* (St. Louis: Chalice Press, 2000); Sharon Ringe, *Jesus, Liberation, and the Biblical Jubilee* (Minneapolis: Fortress Press, 1985); John Yoder, *The Politics of Jesus*, 2nd ed. (Grand Rapids: Eerdmans, 1994), 60–75.

[21] Mark 6:34-44 (LM: January 8 or Tuesday after the Epiphany; RCL: Ord 16B).

with Jesus, there is more than enough food and life.[22] In that remarkable project, *The Saint John's Bible*,[23] this story of the feeding of a great crowd is set next to an illumination in which fish and loaves and fragments of loaves and bread baskets cascade over the pages and around the handwritten text. The very abundance of the many images draws the viewer into the abundance of the story. And yet this rightfully extravagant illumination is subtly marred by solid, dark blue rectangles, obstacles that interrupt the flow of bread and fish off the page into the world.[24] What is it that halts the flow of more than sufficient food for all who dwell on earth? Is it not human greed that obstructs God's feeding of all creatures? Or perhaps it is this: silent indifference, inaction, and an unwillingness to reform the economy of this world that supports the probability of impeded growth in hungry children and early death for the physically vulnerable.

What, then, might Luke be suggesting to the worshiping assemblies in which his gospel is proclaimed? Are the hungry poor the object of God's particular attention in a culture that rewards social value only to those who are economically productive or wealthy? Is it possible that well-to-do members in Lucan assemblies have concluded mistakenly that wealth is a sign of God's blessing? Or have they made the maintenance of wealth into a pursuit that claims their ultimate loyalty, displacing their loyalty to the One who said, "Blessed are you who are hungry now, for you will be filled. . . . Woe to you who are full now, for you will be hungry"? Through canticle, parable, petition, and narrative

---

[22] Mark 6:14-29 (LM: Friday in Fourth Week of the Year; ELW: L 15B; RCL: Pr. 10B).

[23] http://www.saintjohnsbible.org.

[24] Susan Sink, *The Art of The Saint John's Bible: The Complete Reader's Guide* (Collegeville: Liturgical Press, 2013), 234–235.

action, Luke may well be wondering if people who suffer with hunger are actually welcomed into the Christian assembly, into the breaking of the bread. Or perhaps they were excluded, the power of culturally shaped closed meal practices subverting the practice of Jesus. Consider the words of another New Testament author: "If a brother or sister is naked and lacks daily food, and one of you says to them, 'Go in peace; keep warm and eat your fill,' and yet you do not supply their bodily needs, what is the good of that?"[25]

What did the starving woman seek? "For three days now I have had only water and nothing to eat. . . . When I saw you handing out the hosts, those little pieces of white bread, I went to Communion just out of hunger for that little bit of bread."

Sharing Food with Outcasts

Consider, as well, this story narrated in the Synoptic Gospels:

> Jesus went out and saw a tax collector named Levi, sitting at the tax booth; and he said to him, "Follow me." And he got up, left everything, and followed him. Then Levi gave a great banquet for him in his house; and there was a large crowd of tax collectors and others sitting at the table with them. The Pharisees and their scribes were complaining to his disciples, saying, "Why do you eat and drink with tax collectors and sinners?" Jesus answered, "Those who are well have no need of a physician, but those who are sick; I have come to call not the righteous but sinners to repentance."[26]

[25] James 2:15-17; see James 2:14-18 (LM: Ord 24B; ELW: L 23B; RCL: pr. 18B).

[26] Luke 5:27-32; see Matthew 9:9-13 (LM: Ord 10A; ELW: L 10A; RCL: Pr. 5A); Mark 2:13-22 (LM: Saturday in the First Week of the Year and Monday in the Second Week; ELW: L8B; RCL: Pr. 3B).

A casual reading of the story might lead one to assume that Jesus is offering a teaching concerning his mission, a mission directed to sinners and to those who are sick. But, again, one needs to ask why Mark, Matthew, and Luke include this story for the worshiping assemblies addressed in their gospels. What did they mean *then* by the term *sinner*?[27] If one is reading the gospels carefully, it should be clear that Jesus met with opposition throughout his public life, in this case, opposition in the form of grumbling. Why opposition? A good number of New Testament scholars suggest that the culture in which Jesus and his disciples lived was frequently divided into those who were considered observant religious persons (who would claim to be righteous) and those considered nonobservant by choice (for example, worshipers of Roman gods), by condition (mental instability or disease, for example), or by profession (such as imperial tax collectors; prostitutes—women with no living male relative to support them; peasants who had to work when labor was available—thus working on the sabbath). In a region controlled by an oppressive and polytheistic military force, it would not be uncommon to separate people into those who resisted that colonizing power: "insiders" (that is, religiously observant Israelites) and those who were perceived to be outside of this "holy" community (such as impoverished peasants, people perceived as possessed by a troubling spirit, tax collectors, Romans). Anthropologists use the categories of "clean" and "unclean" to describe the common divisions people make between "us" insiders and those perceived to be "out there." Some would suggest that the term *sinner* referred to persons viewed as "unclean," as outsiders.

---

[27] Keep in mind that a doctrine of original sin affecting the whole human race had not yet been elaborated.

Another layer attends this division: to share a meal with others was not a merely utilitarian exercise. Rather, to share food and drink with others was to accept them and, in turn, to be accepted by them as part of their status in society. Sharing a meal implied *a sharing in each other*. Thus, as noted before, rarely does one find a peasant invited to dine as an equal with a landlord or a "holy" religious leader. Impoverished widows did not send dinner invitations to army officers. Funeral workers—"unclean" because they touched the dead—would not be invited to a wedding feast. All three gospels report the story of a woman "of the city" who breaks into a meal hosted by a religious leader and begins to anoint Jesus's feet. His shocked host thinks to himself that if Jesus were truly a prophet he would know what kind of woman she is—a "sinner," an outsider—"and would want nothing to do with her."[28] Imagine the gossip and the possible damage done to Jesus's reputation. Yet, this unnamed woman has shown hospitality to Jesus—something his host has failed to do. And more: she demonstrates genuine love for Jesus and this love shines more brightly and sincerely than any alleged failing on her part. Jesus honors her loving action and thus welcomes her to dinner as a woman with whom he identifies.

"Why do you eat and drink with sinners?" Why do you drink with "outcasts" and thus share their life and social status? Is it possible that Jesus recognizes something deeper in the person or group labeled "sinner" or "unclean," in the person or group perceived to be a poor fit—a misfit—with established custom? Consider, for a moment, the millions of white Christians who demanded separate and inferior dining spaces for black Christians in America's Deep South and in South Africa. Consider the tragic segregation be-

---

[28] Luke 7:36-50 (LM: Ord 11C; ELW: L 11C; RCL: Pr. 6C); Mark 14:3-8 (LM, ELW, RCL: Pass B); Matthew 26:6-13.

tween black and white Christians who, until only recently, celebrated the Mass in separate churches. Consider, if you will, the sequestration of American Indians into reservation churches, their languages, ancient rituals, and spiritual traditions thought to be "unfit" for Christian ritual practice. Consider the many heterosexual Christians in the United States who have refused to share the chalice with homosexual Christians for fear that they would "contract" the "disease" of being gay. Both segregation and the social risk of crossing an invisible boundary into someone's allegedly "inferior" social status marked the world of early Christianity and our world, both made visible in one's meal practice.

While the stories of Jesus eating with tax collectors and honoring a woman who crashed a dinner may well be historical memories, they could also serve as instructions to the Christian communities hearing the stories told in the liturgy. Does Jesus stand against those who are perceived to be "sinners" by Christian religious leaders, or does he ally himself with the socially outcast, understanding how they arrived at this point in their lives and offering them the possibility of transformation? In other words, does he willingly share food and drink and so identify with their lives even when that shared life may cause "respectable" leaders to become offended? In the highly pluralistic world of the ancient Roman Empire, was the opportunity present to divide the Christian assembly into "pure" and "impure"— "godly" and "ungodly"? Perhaps, then, the stories of Jesus eating and drinking with outcasts and the socially marginalized—those who were called "sinners"—served and serve as a critique of Christians who prefer a segregated meal practice, invitations extended only to those who exhibit a certain kind of social status, ethnicity, race, or personal morality. Is it then appropriate to use the Eucharist—a sacrament of grace and love—as a form of punishment by denying it to those who may be perceived as not upholding the churches' teachings? And yet, was it not Jesus who announced this to learned religious leaders: "Tax collectors and prostitutes are entering the kingdom of God ahead of you"?[29] One is reminded of that remarkable scene in Flannery O'Connor's short story "Revelation," in which that judgmental and devoutly religious matron from the Deep South, Mrs. Turpin, beholds a specter in the evening sky:

> A visionary light settled in her eyes. She saw the purple streak in the sky as a vast swinging bridge extending upward from the earth through a field of living fire. Upon it a vast horde of souls were rumbling toward heaven. There were whole companies of white trash, clean for the first time in their lives, and bands of blacks in white robes, and battalions of freaks and lunatics shouting and clapping and leaping like frogs. And bringing up the end of the procession was a tribe of people who she recognized at once as those who, like herself, had always had a little of everything and the God-given wit to use it right . . . They were marching behind the others with great dignity, accountable as they had always been for good order and common sense and respectable behavior. They alone were on key. Yet she could see by their shocked and altered faces that even their virtues were being burned away."[30]

Perhaps there is more to the Eucharist than one's personal encounter with Christ, more than the promise of personal immortality. Perhaps the metaphors expand to include those who struggle with chronic hunger, famine, drought, and starvation. Are the hungry poor welcome into one's assembly, into the Eucharist, or are they simply the objects of one's charity, still distant from the equitable sharing of food and

---

[29] Matthew 21:31.

[30] Flannery O'Connor, "Revelation," in *The Complete Stories* (New York: Farrar, Straus and Giroux, 1946), 508.

drink that rests at the heart of the eucharistic economy? And if hunger for "those little pieces of white bread"—an expression of the growth in chronic hunger across the land—is a viable eucharistic meaning, would it not be incumbent on eucharistic assemblies and their leaders to ask why—why in a land marked by astonishing wealth and boastful of its promise to offer life, to say nothing of happiness—why do children and adults continue to struggle with hunger, continue to form the largest percentage of hungry people among all—*all*—developed nations?

Or this: Is the baptismal unity of the Christian assembly, a unity confirmed and nourished in the eucharistic mystery, actually contradicted when those perceived as outsiders, doubters, dissidents, or as "unworthy," are excluded by an assembly or its leaders for the sake of doctrinal or moral "purity"? One is compelled to ask: Where would the historical Jesus be found: eating and drinking—sharing life and status—with tax collectors and sinners or with those who sit in the seat of judgment?

Chapter Four

The Banquet of God's Vulnerable Creation

In June 1962, *The New Yorker* magazine began to publish a series of articles written by the marine biologist Rachel Carson. These articles drew attention to what Carson considered the dangerous effects of synthetic pesticides, in particular the antimalarial insecticide DDT.[1] In September 1962, the collected articles were published in book form as *Silent Spring*, a title inspired by John Keats, the English Romantic poet, who wrote of withered plants ("sedge") and the silencing of bird song. There were two immediate responses to Carson's book: first, a swift denunciation by the US chemical industry and research scientists at a number of American universities, and second, a growing sense of alarm that eventually reached President John Kennedy, who directed his Science Advisory Committee to investigate Carson's claims. While controversy surrounded her method of investigation, the Advisory Committee vindicated Carson's work—a vindication that led to stricter regulation of chemical pesticides. More than fifty years after the book's publication, *Silent Spring* is viewed by many as the work that accelerated if not gave birth to the modern ecological movement in North America.

---

[1] Dichlorodiphenyltrichloroethane.

One month after the publication of *Silent Spring* and its endorsement by the first Roman Catholic president of the United States, His Holiness Pope St. John XXIII presided at the opening of the Second Vatican Council on October 11, 1962. The first document approved and published by the council, *Sacrosanctum Concilium*, concerned the reform of the liturgy (December 4, 1963). The last document of the council, *Gaudium et Spes*, concerned the engagement of the church with the modern world, with what the Pastoral Constitution referred to as the "hopes and anxieties" of modern people (December 7, 1965). What the council and its many observers could not have imagined in the heady days of ecumenical dialogue that flowed from this commitment to *aggiornamento*[2] would be what we know well today, some fifty years after the publication of *Gaudium et Spes* and *Silent Spring*: ours is a wounded earth suffering the depredations of human-inspired pollution, species extinction, land degradation, and increasing global warming. One, then, wonders: What might be the relationship between the reformed eucharistic liturgy and the palpable hopes and anxieties of people throughout the world regarding the fate of the earth and the suffering of those currently affected by global warming?

Grain from the Field, Fruit of the Vine

At the beginning of each Sabbath and feast day in Jewish households, a form of this blessing is pronounced at table over a wine cup and then a loaf of bread: "You are blessed, Lord our God, King of the universe, you who created the fruit of the vine. . . . You are blessed, Lord our God, King of the universe, you who have brought bread forth from the

---

[2] "Bringing up to date" or "modernizing."

earth."[3] When the gospels narrate Jesus "taking and *blessing*" a wine cup, fish, many loaves or a single loaf of bread,[4] his blessing was not an impromptu exclamation—"I just thank you, Father God, for this beautiful day"—but rather a form of this Jewish prayer of thanksgiving at table for God's gift of fertile land, its grain, and grapes. The Mass of Paul VI introduced a form of this ancient Jewish blessing, a blessing proclaimed during the preparation of the gifts by the presider: "Blessed are you, Lord God of all creation, / for through your goodness we have received / the bread we offer you: / fruit of the earth and work of human hands . . . we have received / the wine we offer you: / fruit of the vine and work of human hands . . ."[5] The *Book of Common Prayer* invites the presider to pray: "O Lord our God, you are worthy to receive glory and honor and power; because you have created all things, and by your will they were created and have their being."[6] One Lutheran rite includes this prayer as the gifts are placed on the altar: "God of all creation, all you have made is good . . . you bring forth bread from the earth and fruit from the vine."[7]

The blessing of God over bread and wine should alert one to the recognition that bread and wine—as well as water, olive oil, flowers, beeswax, incense, stone, wood, glass, silver, gold, cotton, flax, and wool—are gifts of the

[3] See Deiss, *Springtime*, 6, for the reconstruction of this blessing. Scholars note that the blessing was codified after the life of Jesus.

[4] The feeding of the five thousand in Mark 6:30-56; Matthew 14:13-21 (LM: Ord 13B; ELW: L 18A; RCL; Pr. 13A); Luke 9:10-17; John 6:1-13 (LM: Ord 17B; ELW: L 17B; RCL: Pr. 12B); the Last Supper in Mark 14:12-25 (LM, ELW, RCL: Pass B); Matthew 26:17-29 (LM, ELW, RCL: Pass A and HW Sat ABC; LM: HW Wed); Luke 22:7-20 (LM, ELW, RCL: Pass C and CKing C); breaking of bread at Emmaus in Luke 24:13-49 (See Ch. 1, n. 1); and implicit in the giving of bread and fish in John 21:1-19 (LM, ELW, RCL: East 3C).

[5] RM 13, 15.

[6] BCP 377 (Revelation 4:11).

[7] ELW 107.

earth and the work of human hands. The celebration of the Eucharist welcomes these ordinary gifts of earth—the visible form of the sacrament—that communicate the presence of the risen Christ. Or say it this way: there is no such thing as a nonmaterial Eucharist—Spirit is present in and through Matter. Indeed, a sacramental life is a life deeply intertwined with creation and many of its creatures. It should come as no surprise, then, that early and medieval Christians welcomed earth's images and gifts into their eucharistic vocabulary: fish, lambs, and pelicans[8] who give their lives as nourishment to the hungry; aromatic resin burned as incense to honor the eucharistic gifts, the altar, the living and the dead; scented olive oil—chrism—used in the consecration of the altar; the crushed grape and the beaten grain yielding fermented wine and unleavened or leavened bread; the mixing of water with wine to expand the drink or cut the wine for sipping by children and the infirm; the wax created by bees that forms the candles marking the space within which bread and wine become Body and Blood—to say nothing of the towering paschal candle signifying the light of Christ; the flax plant transformed into linen upon which rest paten and chalice; cotton and wool yielding vesture for ministers of the liturgy; silver and gold drawn from earth's depths and transformed into plate and wine cup; stone and wood sheltering the assembly as it gathers for the Supper of the Lamb; flowers, plants, and trees offering a hint of Paradise being restored through the new Adam, the firstborn of all creation. Guided by the movement of the sun and the moon throughout the year, Christian communities mark feasts, fasts, and seasons. One can thus claim that

---

[8] The "pelican in her piety" was a medieval liturgical image: plucking her breast, the pelican mother feeds her young with her blood. See Maurice Dilasser, *Symbols of the Church*, trans. Mary Durkin, OSU, Madeleine Beaumont, and Caroline Morson (Collegeville: Liturgical Press, 1999), 23 and 39.

Christians have welcomed creation and its many creatures into its sacramental rites: Is it possible, then, that Christians have been celebrating a "Mass of Creation" day in and day out for hundreds, if not thousands, of years? Is the feast of earth and its many gifts not set forth in the presence of the assembly on and around the altar?

And yet, this awareness has frequently been obscured by an anthropocentric and, at times, Gnostic and thus earth-escaping sensibility. *Anthropocentric*: humanity is the center of all existence and of utmost value while the earth and all other creatures exist solely for human domination and use or abuse of the earth and its creatures. What does it matter, some ask, if the waters are touched by toxins, the air polluted, the land stripped of its life-giving nutrients, and countless species cease to exist as long as this one species among the many can do whatever it desires to maximize the comfort and wealth of the few while the many suffer the effects of such abuse? *Gnostic*: the assertion—quite lively in Christian history—that matter, materiality, and the body are prisons of the imperishable soul waiting for release at death into an allegedly superior "spiritual" state. One wonders: What was and is the point of the incarnation of the Son of God, his loving desire to be united with all creatures as a breathing, feeling, thinking, eating, drinking, weeping, sleeping, walking, dying, living *body*? Indeed, has this sad emphasis not been underscored in the majestic prayer to the Mother of God that oddly juxtaposes human, bodily existence "in this vale of tears" with the holiness of the female body giving birth to the "fruit of your womb, Jesus"?[9]

---

[9] "Hail, Holy Queen, Mother of mercy, our life, our sweetness, and our hope. To you do we cry, *poor banished children of Eve*. To you do we send up our sighs, *mourning and weeping in this vale of tears*. Turn, then, most gracious Advocate, your eyes of mercy toward us, and after this, *our exile*, show unto to us the blessed fruit of your womb, Jesus. O clement, O loving, O sweet Virgin Mary"; emphasis mine.

Earth-escaping: the conviction that the primary function of Christian faith and the Christian Eucharist is to guide the immaterial soul out of this world into an immaterial and otherworldly existence frequently referred to as heaven, the heavenly country, one's true home. Have Christians missed the remarkable vision narrated by the Seer of Patmos: "I saw the holy city, the new Jerusalem, *coming down out of heaven from God*, prepared as a bride adorned for her husband. And I heard a loud voice from the throne saying: 'See, *the home of God is among mortals.* He will dwell with them; they will be his people, and God himself will be with them.'"[10] Under the influence of end-of-the-world fiction produced by contemporary fundamentalists, one wonders if Christians lost the eschatological vision of God's creative and loving power transforming the earth: "The one who was seated on the throne said, 'See, I am making all things new.'"[11]

A Wounded Earth

In his encyclical on care for the earth and its creatures, Pope Francis writes: "This [earth] cries out to us because of the harm we have inflicted on her by our irresponsible use and abuse of the goods with which God has endowed her. We have come to see ourselves as her lords and masters, entitled to plunder her at will. . . . This is why the earth herself is among the most abandoned and maltreated of our poor."[12] He then narrates the wounds inflicted upon the

---

[10] Revelation 21:2-3 (LM: East 5C; ELW and RCL: East 5C, AllS B, NewY ABC); emphasis mine. See Micah Kiel, *Apocalyptic Ecology: The Book of Revelation, the Earth, and the Future* (Collegeville: Liturgical Press, 2017); and Barbara Rossing, *The Rapture Exposed: The Message of Hope in the Book of Revelation* (New York: Basic Books, 2005), 141–158.

[11] Revelation 21:5.

[12] Pope Francis, *Laudato Si'*, 7.

earth: the poisoning of water, land, and air; the dumping of millions of tons of nonbiodegradable toxic waste without regard for the safety of land, water, and creatures; the loss of biodiversity upon which much life depends; the decreasing quality and quantity of water in many regions as well as the privatization of water for profit, such profit serving corporations and wealthy investors; and most alarming—the warming of earth's climate by human-produced emissions from fossil fuels.[13]

Place this list of threatening forces next to the Eucharist—the banquet of God's creation—and a series of troubling questions emerge. If the celebration of the Eucharist welcomes the gifts of the earth, welcomes nutritious soil and clean water, will preachers, teachers, catechists, and musicians draw attention to this dependency and concomitant Christian responsibility for earth's viability? Or will consideration of the relationship between the Eucharist and earth's gifts be avoided because such discussion might raise uncomfortable questions about "our irresponsible use and abuse"—and thus call into question the lifestyles of all Christians and the occupational choices of some Christians? Will we avoid a difficult discussion of threats to soil and water by "spiritualizing" the Eucharist into nothing more than the promise of eternal life elsewhere?

Would it be ironic if not hypocritical to forbid the addition of tainted water to the wine in the chalice yet remain silent in the presence of water sources fouled by factory effluence, sewage runoff, and agricultural pesticides? In the first book of creation, we read: "The earth brought forth vegetation: plants yielding seed of every kind, and trees of every kind bearing fruit with the seed in it. And God saw that it was good. . . . God said, 'See, I have given you every plant yielding seed that is upon the face of all the earth, and every

---

[13] Francis, *Laudato Si'*, 18–30.

tree with seed in its fruit; you shall have them for food.' "[14] We have claimed here that the Eucharist is dependent upon the seed and vine that will become bread and grape. What, then, of the corporate practice of gaining control over all seed types by claiming "seed patents" and thus producing a monopoly on seeds? Would this practice not prove problematic for Christians who hold that the basic goods that sustain life, among them bread, be shared among the many rather than controlled and hoarded by the few?

Upon entering the church and passing by the baptismal or holy water font, Christians dip their fingers into the water and make the sign of the cross over their bodies. Such a gesture not only signifies the tree of death on which the Lord Jesus was crucified; it also holds forth the tree of life found in the New Jerusalem: "The angel showed me the river of the water of life, bright as crystal, flowing from the throne of God and of the Lamb through the middle of the city. On either side of the river is the tree of life with its twelve kinds of fruit . . . and the leaves of the tree are for the healing of the nations."[15] Is it possible that the one who makes the sign of the cross is leaning into the future, into this vision of clean running water set next to the tree of life, a tree filled with life-giving leaves for the healing of the nations? Is that a vision only of the future? What, then, of the widespread practice of deforestation for the sake of fossil fuel mining, the unsustainable harvesting of timber, and corporate control of farming and ranching? Should Christians not reconsider the mystical vision of the Seer, a vision that accords with what scientists confirm today: that forests and their flora actually contain healing properties

---

[14] Genesis 1:11-12, 29 (LM: EVig ABC; ELW and RCL: Bapt B, EVig ABC, Trin A).

[15] With Ezekiel 47:1, this text forms the antiphon—*Vidi aquam*—sung in the Roman Rite during the *asperges* throughout the Easter season; see Revelation 22:1-2.

as well as the capacity to absorb carbon dioxide that would otherwise float free and contribute to global warming? In other words, the cross, traced on the body before or after receiving Communion: Can it not be for Christians the tree of healing as well as the sign of one's commitment to care for our common home?

Vulnerable People

The onset of industrialization in the eighteenth century was accompanied by the dream of the Enlightenment: the conviction that progress for human well-being would grow to the degree that rational and scientific exploration of life on earth triumphed over what was thought to be the "superstition" of religion. This was a dream—a Western European and then a North American dream—that coincided with the expansion of colonialism and the Doctrine of Discovery: of gaining political and social control over indigenous people and their lands for the sake of the colonizers' economic gain.[16] In the United States, the Doctrine of Manifest Destiny animated the decimation of indigenous communities and their forced sequestration on reservations. Their millennia-old experience of living in harmony with the

---

[16] The commonly called "Doctrine of Discovery" refers to the papal bull promulgated by Alexander VI in May 1493, an ecclesial document that supported Spain's desire to gain exclusive right to the lands "discovered" by Columbus the previous year. The bull, titled *Inter Caetera*, assigned to Spain the right to considerable territorial possessions in the New World and allowed Spain to control any land not inhabited by Catholic Christians. At the same time, the bull promoted the "exaltation" of the Catholic faith and the Christian religion over all other forms of religion. In effect, this "doctrine" served as the foundation of all European claims of control over the land and indigenous people, thus joining together the abuse of land with that of the people. The Episcopal Church, the Evangelical Lutheran Church in America, and other communions as well as a number of Roman Catholic religious orders have repudiated the papal bull and its use in the Doctrine of Manifest Destiny.

natural landscape and its many creatures was utterly ignored by their subjugators. At the same time, the economy of cotton in America's South thrived on the illegal and immoral importation of Africans who were subjected to horrific, impoverishing slavery and the subsequent erasure of their ancestry and cultural gifts.

This pattern of political subjugation for the sake of economic profit—used time and again by all imperial powers[17]—was found throughout much of the world in the nineteenth and twentieth centuries. But this deathly control over subjugated people called into question the dream of progress, for it was clear that "progress" would benefit the well-being of the conquerors alone, not the conquered; indeed, a small coterie of elite North American and Western European families could enjoy tea or sherry on the veranda while Gambians, Guarani, Incans, Indians, Irish, Kenyans, Malaysians, Mayans, Senegalese, Sicilians, and Vietnamese—to name only a few—lived in abject poverty on the other side of walled estates. While many North Americans and Western Europeans hailed the triumph of Reason and Progress, the twentieth century witnessed the unraveling of that dream with the two deadliest conflicts in human history, the creation and use of an atomic weapon with disastrous human and ecological results, the sudden growth of global warming due to accelerating, unregulated fossil fuel emissions, and the first accurate accounting in human history of regional and worldwide poverty.

---

[17] Let us be mindful that this process—colonization through military force for the sake of economic control benefitting the few—was employed in the subjugation of Israel (Roman Palestine or Iudaea) prior to and during the life of Jesus and his early Christian followers. For the internal process of Israelite colonization, see Walter Brueggemann, "Royal Consciousness: Countering the Counterculture," in *The Prophetic Imagination*, 21–38; for Roman colonization at the time of Jesus, see John Dominic Crossan, "Empire and the Barbarism of Civilization," in *God & Empire: Jesus Against Rome, Then and Now* (New York: HarperCollins, 2007), 7–48.

No wonder Pope Francis writes that "the deterioration of the environment and of society affects the most vulnerable people on the planet: 'Both everyday experience and scientific research show that the gravest effects of all attacks on the environment are suffered by the poorest.'"[18] More than three million children throughout the world die annually before reaching their fifth birthday due to polluted water, air, and land.[19] In the United States, 15 million children live in poverty—21 percent of all children—and these children live in some of the most degraded environments in the nation. Neighborhoods of people who struggle with poverty or low income differ radically from the residential enclaves of the middle class and the wealthy. Neighborhoods with little economic, political, or social voice or advantage are frequently found next to freeways, rail yards, factories, refineries, and industrial zones wherein exhaust, toxic effluence, and minute, life-threatening particulates produce respiratory inflammation and disease unknown in wealthier neighborhoods. While households with adequate and more than adequate incomes waste the greatest amount of food, it is the poor in North America and throughout the world—some 1.6 billion people—who struggle daily to secure adequate food for their children and themselves. In this distressing context, Jesus's instruction on how to pray— Give us this day our daily bread—is marked by an urgency known to many struggling people of faith and virtually unknown to others who have sufficient and more than sufficient daily bread.[20] This is to say that Christians live in a

---

[18] *Laudato Si'* 34.

[19] See "Children's Environmental Health," at http://www.who.int/ceh/publications/factsheets/fs284/en/, accessed July 11, 2017.

[20] Matthew 6:9-13 (LM, ELW, RCL: Ash ABC) and Luke 11:2-4 (LM: Ord 17C; ELW L 17C; RCL: Pr. 12C).

world marked by a *tolerated inequity*: "Whenever food is thrown out, it is stolen from the table of the poor."[21]

What, then, of the practice of Jesus? Christian artists and theologians have portrayed him as a Hebrew prophet, learned Jewish rabbi, redeemer of fallen humanity, philosopher of the Gentiles, savior of the world, ruler of the universe, judge of the living and the dead, mystical lover of the soul, reformer of religion, teacher of civic virtues, and one's best friend.[22] As a symbolic figure containing a surplus of meaning, there is a measure of truth in each of these images, though not one of them can hold the fullness of who he is. Distant in time and space from first-century Roman Palestine, most artists, theologians, preachers, and teachers in Christian history have been unaware of or have overlooked his location within the economic and social context of the Galilee. In this regard, the work of social historians of the New Testament is illuminating: they suggest that he was born into a village family marked by subsistence, with Joseph, and perhaps Jesus himself, working as a skilled laborer in the construction of the imperial city of Sepphoris, not far

---

[21] *Laudato Si'* 35–36; Pope Francis discusses a consumerist view of life present in the industrialized regions of the world and one of the most debilitating effects of this view: the emergence of a "throw-away" culture influencing all aspects of life—the environment as "resource" or "object" to be used and frequently abused for human gain, then thrown away; human beings perceived as "unproductive" in a capitalist economy and thus devoid of socially ascribed value: "throw-away people" easily dismissed by those who control the economy.

[22] For helpful overviews of the question, see John O'Grady, *Models of Jesus Revisited* (New York: Paulist Press, 1994); Elizabeth Johnson, *Consider Jesus: Waves of Renewal in Christology* (New York: Crossroad, 1992): Jaroslav Pelikan, *Jesus Through the Centuries: His Place in the History of Culture* (New Haven: Yale University Press, 1999); Thomas Rausch, SJ, *Who Is Jesus? An Introduction to Christology* (Collegeville: Liturgical Press/ Michael Glazier, 2003).

from their home in Nazareth.[23] He was well acquainted with the impoverished lives of peasants who lived in the Galilee, the region of Roman Palestine in which his public ministry was exercised. The vast majority of people he encountered were captive to a tenuous hold on life. Indeed, some who listened to him and recognized his social formation in village life thought his preaching ludicrous.[24] What we do not hear clearly in the gospels is the growth of poverty throughout Roman Palestine under Herod the Great, just prior to the birth of Jesus, and during his life under that great "lover of luxury," Herod Antipas[25]—a growth in destitution that was a significant dimension of the context in which the earliest traditions concerning Jesus were formed.

Is it any wonder, then, that the gospels are filled with encounters between Jesus and despised tax collectors, "sinners" (whose daily occupations or lack of religious observance merited this designation), prostitutes, the working poor, wandering beggars, the chronically sick (marginalized from village or urban communities), and the disabled (perceived as economically unproductive and socially useless)? While Christians have exalted Jesus's disciples as saints and

---

[23] K. C. Hanson and Douglas E. Oakman, *Palestine in the Time of Jesus: Social Structures and Social Conflicts*, 2nd ed. (Minneapolis: Fortress Press, 2008).

[24] Mark 6:1-3 (LM: Ord 14B; ELW: L 14B; RCL: Pr. 9B).

[25] Luise Schottroff and Wolfgang Stegemann, *Jesus and the Hope of the Poor*, trans. Matthew O'Connell (Eugene: Wipf & Stock, 2009), 17. See also Leslie Hoppe, OFM, *There Shall Be No Poor Among You: Poverty in the Bible* (Nashville: Abingdon Press, 2004); Douglas E. Oakman, *Jesus and the Peasants* (Eugene: Cascade Books, 2008), 164–180; Walter E. Pilgrim, *Good News to the Poor: Wealth and Poverty in Luke and Acts* (Minneapolis: Augsburg, 1981). For another view, consider Morten Hørning Jensen, *Herod Antipas in Galilee: The Literary and Archaeological Sources on the Reign of Herod Antipas and Its Socio-Economic Impact on Galilee*, Wissenschaftliche Untersuchungen zum Neuen Testament 2.215 (Tübingen: Mohr Siebeck, 2006).

martyrs, the irony rests in the fact that few of them were persons of economic, political, or social advantage but rather drawn from the many who experienced anxiety and fear that there might be no daily bread tomorrow—men who were subsistence fishermen (Simon/Peter, Andrew, James, and John)[26] and women previously possessed of infirmities and thus socially marginalized (Mary of Magdala, Joanna, and Susanna).[27] Indeed, it was the Galilean mother of Jesus who proclaimed, "My Savior . . . has filled the hungry with good things, and sent the rich away empty."[28] And thus, is it any wonder that when her son has been exalted and distanced from human life as ruler of the universe, the "king of creation," or judge of the living and the dead, the Christian poor of this world have called out to Mary? "We flee to your protection, O holy Mother of God. Despise not our petitions in our need, but deliver us from all dangers, O glorious and blessed virgin."[29]

When the Emperor Constantine legalized the Christian religion in the early fourth century, he provided land and funds to build the first monumental public churches in Rome, Bethlehem, and Jerusalem. In Rome and then throughout the West, the basilica became the model for

[26] Mark 1:14-20 (LM: Ord 3B; ELW and RCL: Epi 3B); see K. C. Hanson, "The Galilean Fishing Economy and the Jesus Tradition," *Biblical Theology Bulletin* 27 (1997): 99–111.

[27] Luke 7:36–8:3 (LM: Ord 11C; ELW: L 11C; RCL: Pr. 6C); see Bruce Malina and Richard Rohrbaugh, *Social-Science Commentary on the Synoptic Gospels* (Minneapolis: Fortress Press, 2003), 256–257. Let us point out that the three women mentioned are credited with supporting Jesus and his reform movement with their funds.

[28] Luke 1:53; see Luke 1:39-56 (LM: Adv 3B, Assum; ELW and RCL: Adv 3A/B, Adv 4B/C).

[29] The *Sub Tuum Praesidium* is the oldest extant prayer addressed to Mary, the earliest manuscript written in Greek. There is conflict over the dating, some placing it in the early 200s and others in the late 300s. See Deiss, *Springtime*, 258n9.

Christian churches: an entryway or narthex, leading worshipers into the nave—the expansive space in which moved the assembly—and then the focal point of the entire space: the altar, centrally located at the opposite end of the entryway. Whether enclosed within a semicircular apse or located on a flat wall, an image of Christ was invariably placed above the altar. As Christian Norberg-Schulz notes, the basilica plan served as a path from the entryway's baptismal pool to the altar. The purpose of this architectural plan, still found in most Western churches today, was to lead the worshiping assembly to the place of encounter with Christ, mediated through bread and wine, his Body and Blood. The architectural plan thus imagined the Christian life as a journey on a path to the sacramental encounter with Christ—the Christ portrayed artistically on the wall above and behind the altar and received materially in the Communion rite—a journey that would then lead worshipers into the world in which the words and actions of the liturgy are intended to animate Christian action in the world.[30]

Who, then, is the Christ encountered in wine cup and bread? Is he an exalted monarch waiting to receive the loyalty of his subjects? Is he the judge of the living and the dead, separating the faithful from the faithless? Is he the savior of all who believe in him? Is he the crucified one, paying the price for human sin or dying in solidarity with all who suffer in this world? An empty cross above the altar helps little in this regard: his humanity, his earthly life, and his passion become virtually invisible.[31] Who is the Christ encountered in wine cup and bread?

---

[30] Christian Norberg-Schulz, *Meaning in Western Architecture*, rev. ed. (New York: Rizzoli, 1980), 73–74.

[31] The loss of the *corpus* or body on the cross can readily contribute to the dematerialization of Christ's humanity. No wonder a plain cross would be favored by Gnostics who taught a spiritualized wisdom that

"Grace tends to manifest itself tangibly," writes Pope Francis.[32] In the presence of a wounded earth in which the growing numbers of people and nations suffer disproportionately from the waste and pollution of wealthy nations, Christ may well come to the worshiping assembly as *Il Poverello*—the Little Poor One—the one who shares the gifts of God's earth with all in need of daily bread, with humans as well as many other creatures.[33] Would Christian perceptions of the Eucharist not be altered were the image of Christ breaking bread among the vulnerable of this earth the artistic framework for the eucharistic action?[34] Christian communions may well cherish a particular understanding of the Eucharist—the eucharistic sacrifice of Christ's Body and Blood; the holy food and drink of new and unending life; the sacrament of forgiveness and salvation. And yet, is there not room in this act of symbolic richness to recognize and follow the One who hears the cry of the poor and the cry of the earth?

---

promised departure from this world and by Manicheans who believed that an evil spiritual force created the world and the body as a deathly prison.

[32] *Laudato Si'* 151–152.

[33] An Italian term often used of St. Francis of Assisi.

[34] Consider the artwork of Cicely Mary Baker, "The Parable of the Great Supper," 1935 (St. George's Anglican Church, Waddon); George Rouault, "Christ and the Poor," 1935 (Art Institute of Chicago); Fritz Eichenberg, "Last Supper," 1952 (*The Catholic Worker*); Eugene Higgins, "The Poor Have the Gospel Preached to Them," 1945; Max Vanka, "Croatian Family Meal with Christ," 1941 (St. Nicholas Croatian Catholic Church, Pittsburgh).

Chapter Five

An Economy of Grace

Mention the word *economy* and what comes to mind? The stock market, money, taxes, trade, recession, investment portfolios, and the cultivation of wealth—all these, coupled with the notion that the economy is the purview of bankers, financial advisers, stockbrokers, accountants, and economists. While economic life seems to be the purview of specialists, the word *economy* has a far humbler origin than what many experience as the complexity of national and global forces over which they seem to have little control. From its origin in Greek *oikos*—the same root for "ecology" and "ecumenical"—an economy is quite simply *a household*, the place within which one dwells; and its cognate, "economics," refers to the manner in which the household is cared for or managed. Whether one lives in an apartment, a single-family dwelling, a nursing home, or a doublewide trailer, one lives in a domestic economy, a household.

Common experience suggests that the household can be organized and guided well—serving the lively flourishing of those who dwell therein, a flourishing rooted in the capacity to share with each other in a gracious and equitable manner. A household, an economy, can also become a nightmare—an experience of abuse, of terrible deprivation as well as the desperate yearning for more and more, of competition, of many conditions attached to the desire for recognition and love. Thus, an economy can serve the well-being of all those who reside therein. And, then this: an economy organized only for the welfare of a few can produce anxiety, corrosive competition, and a sense of failure.

Here are the elements of one household in which human-kind now lives: divorce and death frequently bring forth a contest for property and wealth; citizen groups bemoan tax payments for the well-being of others as the wrongful con-scription of their income; gated residential communities with security forces continue to grow in number; inequity continues between the wealthy few and the many who must work two or more jobs to feed their children; attempts to privatize water for profit are frequently met with resistance in regions with a history of open access to water as a shared good; citizens in twenty industrialized nations can worry about the length of a coffee line while their counterparts in the fifty poorest nations worry about their survival into the next day.

While many in Canada, the United States,[1] and Western Europe may experience little material deprivation, let us keep in mind the larger context: *the household of the world is marked by deathly inequities*, inequities that animate fear, a sense of abandonment, despair, domestic abuse, envy of the well-off, disdain for the poor, hoarding, violent crime, and regional conflicts. It is the experience of life in a material economy that sanctions the vigorous pursuit of capital by individuals, multinational corporations, financial services, medical research institutions, the construction industry, agribusiness, and many healthcare institutions, all of which

---

[1] Since 1930, poverty rates in the United States have exceeded those of other industrialized nations. In 2015, 43 million Americans were living in poverty, including 2.8 million children. As of 2017, 50 percent of the US population qualifies as "poor" or "low income." See https://poverty.ucdavis.edu/faq/what-current-poverty-rate-united-states.

influence access to what every human being needs in order to survive: shelter, food, water, clothing, labor, and medical care. Its religious counterpart is the "gospel of prosperity" loudly preached in the United States, as well as the claim that the accrual of wealth is a sign of God's blessing. Indeed, it was Max Weber, German sociologist and economic theorist, who suggested that the many Protestant groups influenced by the followers of John Calvin were active contributors to an economic system that rewards the accrual of wealth as a sign of divine blessing and views the poor—not "blessed" by God—with punitive regard.[2] One wonders if this is the household in which Christians wish to live.

---

[2] Max Weber, *The Protestant Ethic and The Spirit of Capitalism*, trans. Peter Baehr and Gordon Wells (New York: Penguin Books, 2002), 32–36. While the claim of God's double predestination can be attributed to John Calvin, *he did not promote the notion that one's personal wealth is a sign of God's election or blessing*, a claim that emerged among his followers. For the assertion that Calvin's followers came to view the poor with punitive regard, consider the work of Sigurn Kahl, "The Religious Roots of Modern Poverty Policy: Catholic, Lutheran, and Reformed Protestant Traditions," in the *Archives Européennes de Sociologie* 46, no. 1 (March 2005): 91–126. Kahl examines three different views of religion and social assistance that emerged in the sixteenth century. Since Catholics did not stigmatize poverty—members of religious orders made vows of poverty or simplicity of life, and many saints were well-known ascetics—the poor were valued and assisted by religious orders as well as aristocratic sodalities sponsored by the Society of Jesus, the Jesuits. Lutherans did not ascribe spiritual value to poverty but did view the poor as people who needed assistance, recognizing that forces beyond the control of individuals or families drove people into poverty. When religious life—the center of social assistance for over one thousand years—was suppressed for theological reasons, Lutherans established poor relief as a congregational and municipal responsibility. The Reformed tradition differed from the previous two in that the followers of Calvin came to view financial prosperity as a sign of God's election. In an economy marked by the rapid expansion of merchant capitalism, prosperity was viewed as divine blessing and hard work was prized. What then of the poor? They needed to work in workhouses and give evidence of their "worthiness" to receive

The Economy of God

While this economy is one that many throughout the world take for granted—because they have been raised within its influence and assume its "normality"—is it the only one available to Christians who gather to celebrate the Eucharist? Consider, then, the elements of another story, elements that shape another household. "I have given you every plant yielding seed that is upon the face of all the earth, and every tree with seed in its fruit; you shall have them for food . . . to everything that has the breath of life, I have given every green plant for food."[3] To the primal human beings—and thus to all human beings—as well as all other creatures, the Creator gives food freely. Of course, this offer assumes human care for earth's gifts as becomes clear when, in the second creation story, "tilling and keeping the garden" are cited as human responsibilities.[4] As with the first creation story, one hears in the second story the same offer: "You may eat freely of every tree in the garden."[5] What does this mean but that God provides nourishment for all creatures, not just human beings, and does so prior to the primal parents' act of disobedience and their children's act of violence, the murder of Abel by Cain? In other words, human hunger cannot be associated with human failings. To experience hunger and to seek nourishment is not a moral failure or a sign of sin; it is simply one dimension of creaturely existence. While tilling and keeping becomes

---

social benefits. No work, no assistance—and little awareness of the conditions that promote poverty and the ways in which a permanent class of low-income or poor people serve the interests of others, frequently as a source of cheap labor.

[3] Genesis 1:29-30; see Genesis 1:1–2:4a (LM, ELW, RCL: EVig ABC; ELW and RCL: Trin A; Bapt B).

[4] Genesis 2:15.

[5] Genesis 2:16.

"sweaty toil" when the primal human beings leave the garden,[6] the divine offer of adequate nourishment for all creatures does not end.

Once freed from impoverished slavery in Egypt, the Hebrew people enter the wilderness with little food and drink. Their anxiety leads them to beg for a return to miserable servitude and oppressive inequality: we would rather be enslaved and fed by pharaoh than dependent on God as a free people. It is a startling admission: "If only we had meat to eat! We remember the fish we used to eat in Egypt for nothing, the cucumbers, the melons, the leeks, the onions, and the garlic."[7] Their despair and complaint lead their divine Provider to "rain bread from heaven" but with this significant injunction: "Gather as much of it as each of you needs"—not as much as you desire. Nonetheless, some gathered more and some less, but when the manna, this "bread from heaven," was measured "those who had gathered much had nothing left over and those who had gathered little had no shortage: they gathered as much as each of them needed."[8]

Skeptical rejection of this "miracle" or well-intentioned explanations of how manna might be "an insect's carbohydrate-rich secretion" seem to miss the point: there is sufficient food for the entire community, for women and men, young and old, healthy and infirm. What the writer presents is an economy, a way of caring for this wandering household. Thus their divine Provider teaches them that the world of God's creating is marked not by scarcity but abundance, with enough for everyone. The challenge is this:

[6] Genesis 3:17-19.

[7] Numbers 11:4-6 (LM: Monday in the Eighteenth Week of the Year; ELW: L 26B; RCL: Pr. 21B).

[8] Exodus 16:16-18: See Exodus 16:2-15 (LM: Ord 18B; ELW: L 25A; RCL: Pr. 20A).

Will individuals and communities restrain their pursuit for more and more and live within limits that will make access to God's abundance possible?[9] For we see in this oft-overlooked and rarely preached narrative another dimension of the economy of God, one in which God's abundance —water, manna, and quail—ensures that each person has sufficient to live. But one wonders: Is even the mention of "limits" or "limitations" received as absurd in a world where the drive to consume more and more is constantly promoted and considered a mark of "success"?[10]

"O Lord my God, you are very great . . .You cause the grass to grow and plants for people to cultivate, to bring forth food from the earth, wine to gladden . . . and bread to strengthen the human heart. These all look to you to give them their food in due season . . . when you open your hand, they are filled with good things."[11] Here the psalmist praises God as the One who continually cares for all creatures, among them human beings. Rather than view the creating power and presence of God as a single act of the past—as did the followers of Deism in early European American history[12]—the psalmist underscores the scriptural

[9] See Ched Myers, *The Biblical Vision of Sabbath Economics* (Ventura: Tell the Word, 2002).

[10] See John de Graaf, Thomas Naylor, and David Wann, *Affluenza*, 3rd ed. (San Francisco: Berrett-Koehler, 2014).

[11] Psalm 104:1, 14, 15, 27, 28 (See Ch. 3, n. 17).

[12] Under the influence of the Enlightenment and, in particular, Newtonian-inspired science, Deists posited a reluctant belief in a higher being who brought into existence and set in motion the universe as a remarkable and vast "mechanism" that continues to operate through natural law. One gains the impression from the Deists that once the world is brought into existence, the higher being simply disappears. Such a view animated the scientific exploration of the earth while denying the ongoing presence of the God of Israel and Jesus in human life and history. Reason alone was sufficient to explore, describe, and control the earth and its many creatures.

conviction that God is always engaged in the work of "bringing forth food from the earth . . . and filling all creatures with good things." As the Reformer Martin Luther wrote: "God remains with his creation, is effective in it, continually allows for new animals and human beings to be born, and continually grants new beginnings and in this way preserves creation. God's *conservatio*, God's sustaining of creation, is, to be sure, a sign of his abiding goodness as the creator."[13] The psalm underscores the generosity of God who, through the gifts of the earth, continues to give food—life—to all creatures. There is no sense that some creatures receive more than others; there is no hint of discrimination. Rather, each receives what is needed to flourish: "*all* look to you . . . and are filled with good things."

If there is any truth in the claim that through the agency of creation, God provides abundant food and drink for all creatures, what prevents living into that claim? Why does the story of inequity, of "scarcity"—and the suffering it produces—seem to be the one that is accepted by many and resisted by few? No doubt there may well be a good number of factors, but one in particular has received considerable attention in the history of Christianity. In the Benedictine Abbey Church of Sainte-Marie-Madeleine (St. Mary Magdalene) in Vézelay, France, the careful observer will find a supporting column that bears the figure of a man holding two large bags of gold coin: so heavy are the bags, his shoulders are bent over and his mouth is opened wide, as if he were hungering for more.[14] He is pictured here as the

---

[13] As quoted by Johannes Schwanke, "Luther on Creation," in *Harvesting Martin Luther's Reflections on Theology, Ethics, and the Church*, ed. Timothy Wengert (Grand Rapids: Eerdmans, 2004), 82.

[14] For the image: http://www.medart.pitt.edu/menufrance/vezelay /capitals/vezcap45.html. See Richard Newhauser, *The Early History of Greed: The Sin of Avarice in Early Medieval Thought and Literature* (Cam-

embodiment of *Avaritia*, the vice of greed: the inordinate attachment to and desire for increased wealth, for material possessions.[15] Indeed, for ancient and medieval Christians, the yearning for more material goods than one needs was regarded not only as a moral evil but also as an addictive power: having sufficient to sustain life is never enough; the craving for more leads to the acquisition of more land, more money—the craving for more becomes a "god" who controls one's desires and relationships. Though he is in pain from holding bags of gold, *Avaritia* will not let go of them: he seems incapable of discerning the source of his own suffering. Indeed, this remarkable power has made him blind to others and their needs. And this, too: he is alone. There is no spouse, no child, no parent, no sibling, and no coworker who joins him in the odious work of carrying bags laden with coins. Again, he is alone: his pursuit is solely for himself. His gaping jaws allow no one else to join him in consuming whatever he desires. Of course, what he fails to recognize is that, in the end, he is consuming himself: the plight of every addict. No wonder medieval preachers, artists, theologians, and catechists linked the personification of *Avaritia* with Luke's parable of Dives, the rich man, and Lazarus[16] as well as the Mosaic commandments that govern social relationships: "You shall not commit adultery. You shall not steal . . . you shall not covet your neighbor's

---

bridge: Cambridge University Press, 2000); Newhauser also includes a discussion of greed in the sermons of early Christian preachers.

[15] Of the seven cardinal vices or deadly sins—greed, lust, gluttony, envy, wrath, sloth, and pride—the first four deal with an inordinate desire for more. For the classic treatment of the vices, see Thomas Aquinas, *Summa Theologica*, Ia–IIae, Q 84, accessible at http://www.sacred-texts .com/chr/aquinas/summa/; for a more recent and engaging examination of the vices, see Rebecca DeYoung, *Glittering Vices: A New Look at the Seven Deadly Sins and Their Remedies* (Ada, MI: Brazos Press, 2009).

[16] Luke 16:19-31 (LM: Ord 26C; ELW: L 26C; RCL: Pr. 21C).

house; you shall not covet your neighbor's wife . . . or anything that belongs to your neighbor."[17]

But do only individuals caught in the grip of avarice obstruct God's abundance? Are there larger forces that promote indifference to others, an unwillingness to limit one's desires so that others might simply live? Consider the public ministry of the prophet Amos in the kingdom of Israel during the eighth century BCE, a ministry directed to the entire nation: "Hear this word that the Lord has spoken against you, O people of Israel, against the whole family that I brought up out of the land of Egypt."[18] In his observation of the economic and social condition of Israel, Amos discerns what modern theologians refer to as "social sins" or "systemic evils" that have become normalized in groups or institutions.[19] What does Amos observe and condemn? When the poor cannot pay bloated levies on shelter or land, they are sold into debt slavery: "They sell the righteous for silver, and the needy for a pair of sandals."[20] They have no regard for the afflicted and "push them out of the way."[21] The elite classes drink fine wine in the presence of God—yet wine produced by impoverished laborers. Amos observed the common practice of inflating prices on food sold to the poor, only deepening their impoverishment and increasing their suffering in times of economic instability. In legal proceedings, those charged with the administration of justice

---

[17] Exodus 20:14-15, 17; see Exodus 20:1-17 (LM, ELW, RCL: Lent 3B; ELW: L 27A; RCL: Pr. 22A).

[18] Amos 3:1.

[19] See Daniel Finn, "What Is a Sinful Social Structure?" in *Theological Studies* 77 (2016): 136–164; Cynthia Moe-Lobeda, *Resisting Structural Evil: Love as Ecological-Economic Vocation* (Minneapolis: Fortress Press, 2013), 49–82; William Stringfellow, *The Politics of Spirituality* (Louisville: Westminster John Knox, 1984; Eugene: Wipf & Stock, 2013).

[20] Amos 2:6.

[21] Amos 2:7.

"have turned the judicial system into a bitter pill for the poor."[22] Michael Barré considers the underlying reason for this condemnation the utter disregard by the unrighteous rich for the institutions of justice founded in the covenant between God and Israel: the elite of Israel actually oppose the laws that prevent them from defrauding the poor.[23]

The prophet's anger is directed, in particular, toward the "notables" of the nation, their indifference to the suffering they have caused and the withholding of their excess from those in need: they refuse to share any of their abundance with their fellow citizens. While the destitute live in sweltering valleys, the elite of Israel build their summer homes on the region's hilltops in order to capture the cool breeze from the sea. Of these, says the LORD, "I will tear down the summer house; and the houses of ivory shall perish."[24] "Alas for those who lie on beds of ivory, and lounge on their couches, and eat lambs from the flock, and calves from the stall; who sing idle songs to the sound of the harp . . . who drink wine from bowls, and anoint themselves with the finest oils, but are not grieved over the ruin of Joseph!"[25]

When worship of the Creator and Redeemer—the author of the covenant and its commandments establishing "right" social relationships—is embodied in just relationships, there one discerns authentic love of God and love of neighbor: liturgy and ethics are inextricably linked. But such is not the case in Israel. Preaching the word of the LORD, Amos condemns *worshipers* who disregard and even scorn the social implication of worship: they fail to recognize that the

---

[22] Michael Barré, "Amos," in *The New Jerome Biblical Commentary* (NJB), ed. Raymond Brown, SS, Joseph Fitzmyer, SJ, and Roland Murphy, OCarm (Englewood Cliffs, NJ: Prentice Hall, 1990), 213.

[23] Barré, "Amos," 213.

[24] Amos 3:15.

[25] Amos 6:4-6; see Amos 6:1-7 (LM: Ord 26C; ELW: L 26C; RCL: Pr. 21C). The mention of Joseph is a reference to Israel.

social practices in which they engage—corrupting practices directed at members of their own community—negate the loyalty they appear to offer in worship of the Creator and Redeemer.[26] "I hate, I despise your festivals, and I take no delight in your solemn assemblies. Even though you offer me your burnt offerings and grain offerings, I will not accept them. . . . Take away from me the noise of your songs; I will not listen to the melody of your harps. But let justice roll down like waters, and righteousness like an ever-flowing stream."[27]

Jesus the Prophet of God's Economy

While the gospel writers employ a variety of titles in their portrayal of Jesus—Messiah and Son of David (Matt 1:1), Son of God (Mark 1:1), Savior, Christ, and Lord (Luke 2:11), Word of God (John 1:1)—there is common agreement among them that he was a prophet in the line of the classical prophets of Israel: "This is the prophet Jesus from Nazareth" (Matt 21:11); "Prophets are not without honor, except in their hometown" (Mark 6:4); "Jesus of Nazareth was a prophet mighty in word and deed" (Luke 24:19); "Sir, I see that you are a prophet" (John 4:19). Let us recall that a

---

[26] "Loopholes in the U.S. tax system and dysfunctional politics enable those most able to bear the cost of the economic safety nets designed to protect the poor to pay the least amount proportionally," Robert Ellis, "Amos Economics," in *Review and Expositor* 107 (2010): 463–512, as quoted in Michael Ufok Udoekpo, *Rethinking the Prophetic Critique of Worship in Amos 5 for Contemporary Nigeria and the USA* (Eugene: Pickwick Publication, 2017), 128.

[27] Amos 5:21-24; see Amos 5:18-24 (ELW: L 32A; RCL: Pr. 27A). Given the prominence of this text in the history of Christian liturgy and Christian social ethics, it is perplexing to observe its absence from the Sunday readings in the *Lectionary for Mass*. It is the appointed reading in LM for Wednesday in the Thirteenth Week of the Year.

prophet does not predict the future but rather proclaims or enacts a message from God within a specific context in the present. The prophet's action or speech is an orientation to the immediate future—right now, tomorrow morning—that draws people and leaders toward their fundamental relationship with God and with each other: "Love the LORD your God" (Deut 6:5) and "Love your neighbor as yourself" (Lev 19:18).[28] But use of the word *love* may differ from conventional understandings of the term, for when Jesus speaks about love of God and neighbor, the Greek term of the New Testament text is *agapeseis*, from *agape*: love as passionate commitment to the well-being of others. This is not erotic love (*eros*) or love as friendship (*philia*) but love as action that benefits the welfare, the *salvus*, the health of others.[29] It is a term that also describes the love God holds for all God creates: For God so loved (*egapesen*) the world (*cosmon*).[30]

"O LORD our God, when you open your hand, your creatures are filled with good things."[31] When the psalmist gives thanks for the abundance flowing from God, through the earth, to all creatures, he is not only making a theological claim—God is committed to the welfare of all that God creates—but also an economic one, economic in its original sense: God's continuing care for all who dwell in the household of the earth. This recognition is no new thing in the history of Christianity, though the erosion of memory that

[28] Matthew 22:34-40; see Matthew 22:34-46 (LM: Ord 30A; ELW: L 30A; RCL: Pr. 25A); Mark 12:28-34 (LM: Ord 31B; ELW: L 32B; RCL: Pr. 27B); Luke 10:25-27 (LM: Ord 15C; ELW: L 15C; RCL: Pr. 10C).

[29] Latin *salvus* and *salvatio*: being whole or safe, being rescued from a dire situation.

[30] John 3:16—that is, God's passionate commitment to the well-being or welfare of the cosmos, to the earth and all its creatures.

[31] Psalm 104:28.

characterizes American culture[32] might explain widespread ignorance of this *leitmotif*, of God's management of God's economy, God's care for all who dwell in God's household.

We see such care embodied in the actions and words of Jesus, the prophet of this economy. Luke narrates one story of Jesus that appears in all four gospels, a sign to the contemporary assembly that this memory held a notable position in the oral and written traditions that were used in the creation of the gospels.[33]

> The day was drawing to a close, and the twelve came to [Jesus] and said, "Send the crowd away, so that they may go into the surrounding villages and countryside, to lodge and get provisions; for we are here in a deserted place." But he said to them, "You give them something to eat." They said, "We have no more than five loaves and two fish—unless we are to go and

---

[32] I am indebted to my colleague Dr. Patricia O'Connell Killen, American Church historian, for this insight on *memory erosion*. During the late eighteenth and throughout the nineteenth centuries, European American colonization and expansion across North America was made possible, in part, by the promise that one could forget one's past and start anew in this land. To be sure, it was a cultural promise reinforced by the Christian conviction that God forgives the "sins of the past" and provides a fresh start for the repentant Christian. Millions of immigrants were prompted to leave their homelands and travel to North America so they could escape war, persistent crop failure, famine, and economic collapse *in order to find adequate food through labor*. That expansion was aided in the twentieth century by the acceptance of South and East Asian and then African immigrants. All these were expected, however, to assimilate into American culture—a culture in its origin shaped by northern European Protestants—and "forget" their native heritage. What is infrequently taught in American schools is the subjugation and starvation of the indigenous population. That Africans were forced into slavery during the late eighteenth and nineteenth centuries to serve the profit economy of cotton remains the "wound" that has not yet been fully acknowledged and has not been healed through national repentance and reparation to African Americans and American Indians.

[33] Luke 9:10-17; Matthew 14:13-21; Mark 6:30-44; John 6:1-13.

buy food for all these people." For there were about five thousand men. And he said to his disciples, "Make them sit down in groups of about fifty each." They did so and made them all sit down. And taking the five loaves and the two fish, he looked up to heaven, and blessed and broke them, and gave them to the disciples to set before the crowd. And all ate and were filled. What was left over was gathered up, twelve baskets of broken pieces.

In the history of Christianity, preachers and teachers, scholars and lay readers have viewed the narrative in various and often conflicting manners: as a miraculous intervention in the laws of nature; as a fabulous and thus implausible tale viewed through the rationalist assumptions of the Enlightenment; as a spiritualizing lesson, not about food for hungry people, but about hungering for God; as a foreshadowing of the Last Supper with strong eucharistic overtones. For modern interpreters of the story, the temptation is ever present to "explain," often erroneously, how a small amount of food can feed so many (for example, "everyone shared what they had with others"). Such attempts tend to miss the question: Why do all four evangelists include this story, a story to be read aloud in late first-century worshiping assemblies? Does one discern here an invitation or instruction to Christian worshiping assemblies?

What should not be overlooked is the evangelists' often subtle but clear invocation of narratives that appear in the Hebrew Scriptures and thus in the memory of those familiar with the stories of Israel. Luke, with other evangelists, would have his readers remember the prophet Elisha, successor to Elijah. In a time of famine, Elisha encounters a man bringing an offering of twenty barley loaves as thanksgiving to God for a good harvest. But Elisha instructs him, "Give it to the people and let them eat" (2 Kgs 4:42). Elisha's servant does not understand how twenty loaves can possibly feed one hundred people. Elisha repeats the instruction, noting that the LORD promises that some will be left over. Indeed, all ate of the bread and, indeed, there was some left over.[34] What does the prophet demonstrate? With God, there is abundance rather than scarcity. But also this: "In the Bible, famine is understood not just as an unfortunate natural disaster but as the result of human economic systems of greed."[35] What one recognizes in the Elisha account is a liberal distribution of bread—symbol of nourishment—so that all might live, *a prophetic action* that implicitly criticizes economic systems that fail to respond to fundamental human need.

Luke also notes that Jesus, his disciples, and a large crowd were gathered in a deserted place. Here Luke invokes the memory of escape from Egyptian oppression and God's two wilderness feedings directed through Moses (Exod 16:1-36; Num 11:1-35).[36] Standing behind Jesus and the large crowd are Moses and Elisha, prophets who directed the gathering of food sufficient to feed everyone who was hungry. This claim, however, is not spiritualized hyperbole: the societies in which Elisha and Jesus lived were marked by widespread poverty and hunger due to the control of agricultural land by "notables," by colonizers, or by wealthy elites: "The narrow margin between subsistence and starvation is everywhere attested in the biblical literature (Deut. 15:11; Mark 14:7 and par.). Biblical law and moral injunctions were generally phrased to preserve the status of poor Israelites or poor Christians within the total covenant community."[37] What was "miraculous" to the many hungry poor was that

---

[34] 2 Kings 4:42-44 (LM: Ord 17B; ELW: L 17B; RCL: Pr. 12B).

[35] Myers, *Sabbath Economics*, 48.

[36] Exodus 16:2-15 (LM: Ord 18B; ELW; L 25A; RCL: Pr. 20A); Numbers 11:4-29 (LM: Monday in the Eighteenth Week of the Year; ELW: L 26B; RCL: Pr. 21B).

[37] Oakman, *Jesus and the Peasants*, 67.

a prophet had arisen among them and offered an economic practice rooted in the ancient vision of God's desire to nourish God's creatures with adequate food and drink, *an economy of grace,* an economic system responsive first to human need rather than to the wealth interests of elites or notables.

Rather than interpreting the feeding of five thousand first as a foreshadowing of the Last Supper or the church's Eucharist, is this not a story of thanksgiving, of *eucharistia,* for the One who breaks through an economy of scarcity controlled by the few and organizes his incredulous and apathetic disciples to distribute bread and fish, core elements in the ancient peasant diet, so that all might be nourished? He engages in the management of the household so that no one goes without earth's gifts, freely given by a generous God. And, thus, is this story not an implicit criticism of any economy, including ancient Rome's, controlled by the few for the benefit of the few?

The thirty-third chapter of the Rule of St. Benedict asks whether monks living in community should consider anything their own. Benedict responds quite clearly: "This vice in particular must be torn up by the roots . . . that anyone should consider anything personal property . . . *Let all things be common to all,* as Scripture says, *so that no one may* presume *to call* anything his own."[38] Benedict's scriptural reference is to the Acts of the Apostles: "Now the whole group of those who believed were of one heart and soul, and no one claimed private ownership of any possessions, but everything they owned was held in common."[39]

---

[38] Terence Kardong, OSB, *Benedict's Rule: A Translation and Commentary* (Collegeville: Liturgical Press, 1996), 273–278, but note Kardong's caution regarding Benedict's adaptation of his quotation from the Acts of the Apostles.

[39] Acts 4:32-35 (LM, ELW, RCL: East 2B): see the illumination that accompanies this text in *The Saint John's Bible* with commentary by Sink, "Life in Community," in *The Art of the Saint John's Bible,* 275–278.

While some scholars suggest that this description of the early community of Christ followers is more wishful thinking than historical fact,[40] others argue that "holding things in common" was not unusual: the pooling of resources for group goals was called *koinōnia* in Greek (*societas* in Latin) and translated as "fellowship"—fellowship not as church reception or coffee hour but as the gathering of goods for common use and benefit.[41] Was this "sharing of things in common" at the "direction" of the apostles a new incarnation of the economy of grace enacted by Jesus—"You give them something to eat"—an economy of redistribution for the many that stood in stark contrast to Rome's economy of hoarding by the few, Rome's "disaster economy" that continues in many parts of the world today?

The worshiping assembly stands close to the altar table. And this, too: the worshiping assembly stands within two economies at the same time. Will we ever be free of our cultural habituation in acquisitiveness, of the grasping hand that wants more? Perhaps not. After all, it is in the very air that many if not most of us have been breathing from the moment of birth. And, thus, we should expect a struggle as we seek to be *a bit more* or *much more free* of the economy that whispers, "Get what you can while you can and protect yourself from insecurity." But, then, isn't the call to repentance, isn't the call to leave behind one way of living in this world for another way of living at the very heart of the

[40] The Lucan allusion to "freewill offerings [that] nurture the 'golden age' impression of the apostolic era [is] not unrelated to Hellenistic visions of primal days and political utopias," Richard Dillon, "Acts of the Apostles," in *The New Jerome Biblical Commentary*, 738; "The first years in Jerusalem are idealized [by Luke] as the time when Christians were of one mind," Raymond Brown, SS, in his *Introduction to the New Testament*, 286–287.

[41] Bruce Malina and John Pilch, *Social Scientific Commentary on the Book of Acts* (Minneapolis: Fortress Press, 2008), 46.

preaching of Jesus? "Repent, for the kingdom of God is at hand." And isn't that call at the very heart of proclaiming the good news of the kingdom today? The assembly stands close to the altar table where God's economy of grace is enacted and enlarged by narratives that course through the church's holy book. Here is the challenge: to recognize the Mass, the Eucharist, as an incarnation of the economy of God practiced by Jesus of Nazareth, and then to lean into this practice of caring for the household. For some, such an invitation would be nothing less than an unexpected and astonishing experience of the open and generous hand.

Chapter Six

Holding All Things in Common

Patronal and Communal Meal Practices

Scripture scholars suggest that two types of meals were practiced throughout the Roman Empire at the time of Jesus and the emergence of the movement that claimed his name: a *patronal* meal and a *communal share* meal.[1] A patronal meal was and is sponsored by a host, a patron, who extends invitations to guests; who decides where guests will be seated in light of their importance to the host; who arranges for the preparation and serving of the meal by persons other than the host; who welcomes the guests at the beginning of the meal and bids them farewell at the threshold of the home or hall. Implicit in the patronal meal is the evidence of some measure of wealth, large or small, sufficient for a man or

---

[1] Other types of meals (funerary or municipal, for example) were kept as well. Here we focus on two that informed the Christian tradition. The patronal and communal traditions are distinguished and discussed in John Dominic Crossan, *The Birth of Christianity: Discovering What Happened in the Years Immediately After the Execution of Jesus* (San Francisco: Harper San Francisco, 1998), 423–444; see also Robert Jewett, "Tenement Churches and Pauline Love Feasts," in *Quarterly Review* 14 (1994): 43–58; the excellent summary by Jerome Neyrey, SJ, "Reader's Guide to Meals, Food and Table Fellowship," at https://www3.nd.edu/~jneyrey1/meals.html; Graydon Snyder, "Food and Meals," *Inculturation of the Jesus Tradition: The Impact of Jesus on Jewish and Roman Cultures* (Harrisburg: Trinity Press, 1999), 129–174.

woman to pay the cost of food and drink for a group in his or her home.[2] The patronal meal was held for many reasons but at least for this: to make visible the relationship between the patron-host and guests who were dependent on the host (such as spouse, children, relatives, servants, business associates).[3]

Modern readers gain a glimpse of the patronal meal in the Gospel of Luke: "When Jesus noticed how the guests chose the places of honor, he told them a parable. 'When you are invited by someone to a wedding banquet, do not sit down at the place of honor, in case someone more distinguished than you has been invited by your host; and the host who invited both of you may come and say to you, "Give this person your place," and then in disgrace you would start to take the lowest place.' "[4] This is the advice offered by the Lucan Jesus to his listeners, the worshiping assembly addressed in this gospel: find the lowest place and sit there—"for all who exalt themselves will be humbled, and those who humble themselves will be exalted."[5]

[2] For women hosts in house churches, see Ute Eisen, *Women Officeholders in Early Christianity: Epigraphical and Literary Studies*, trans. Linda Maloney (Collegeville: Michael Glazier/Liturgical Press, 2000); Carolyn Osiek and Margaret MacDonald, *A Woman's Place: House Churches in Earliest Christianity* (Minneapolis: Fortress Press, 2005); *Women & Christian Origins*, ed. Ross Kraemer and Rose D'Angelo (New York: Oxford University Press, 1999).

[3] Scholars who have contributed to the social scientific study of the context in which Christian writings were created and who offer commentary on the New Testament will frequently refer to the God of Israel and Jesus as a "patron," and at times suggest that Jesus was the "broker" of the reign of God. See "Patronage," in *The Handbook of Biblical Social Values*, ed. John Pilch and Bruce Malina (Peabody, MA: Hendrickson Publications, 1998), 151–155.

[4] Luke 14:7-9; see Luke 14:1-14 (LM: Ord 22C; ELW: L 22C; RCL: Pr. 17C).

[5] Luke 14:11.

One wonders if his exhortation was less about face-saving etiquette and more a criticism of a culturally accepted stratification based on economic class and physical health. For, indeed, such divisions were clearly visible in patronal meals, yet such discriminations were alien to the ministry of Jesus, who was criticized for sharing food and drink with "undesirables," with tax collectors and prostitutes.

The patronal meal continues in the world today. One sees it clearly at wedding dinners, award ceremonies, many holiday meals, and state banquets hosted by political leaders. Perhaps one encounters it, to some degree, in churches. While the presider may not decide seating arrangements for participants, the practice of processions that include only the presider and other ministers, the practice of welcoming people to worship with a cheery "good morning," the practice of the presider and other ministers seated in chairs different if not more elaborate from those of the assembly, and the practice of the presider greeting people at the door as they leave can give the clear impression that the presider is the "patron" in the presider's "house," in spite of the best efforts to promote the "priesthood of the baptized."[6] Indeed,

---

[6] It can be surprising for some to discover that for close to 1,500 years Christians did not sit in pews during the liturgy. There is evidence that *the assembly moved together with its ministers* into the church, to a place for the readings and sermon, to the altar, and then, together, out the doors. The entrance psalm, gradual psalm/alleluia verse, offertory psalm, and communion psalm hold the memory of *physically moving throughout the space* while singing. For contemporary examples of church spaces in which the assembly can move to and around symbolic centers, consider the Episcopal Cathedral of Philadelphia (http://www.philadelphia cathedral.org) and St. Spiridon Orthodox Cathedral in Seattle (http:// www.saintspiridon.org). By the thirteenth century, benches were placed against church walls so that nursing mothers, the physically challenged, and the elderly could sit when needed. It was the Protestant Reformation with its emphasis on preaching that prompted the creation of church spaces in which stationary side benches became movable pew benches— pews that would in time become locked in place, rendering the assembly incapable of any movement other than entering and leaving the pew

the practice of restricting those who may commune can be received as discrimination between "higher" and "lower" places in the assembly, between insiders and outsiders. In those churches where wafers (hosts) and wine are housed in a sacristy, it will appear that the presider or an unseen worker provides "food and drink."

Another practice came to prominence during the public life of Jesus: the communal share meal, forerunner of the potluck supper. In this early Christian practice, each person brought to the table what he or she could bring; if one had little or nothing to offer, a participant could always assist in preparations before the meal began or in cleaning up after it ended. The significance of this meal type grows as we remember that the ancient Roman economy was sustained by the physical labor of peasants taxed severely by Rome, that the Roman Empire was a *slave empire* in which much labor was accomplished by indentured servants, colonized slaves and their offspring, and children sold into slavery. It should not surprise us that many early Christians were of lower economic status. Recall, then, that until the early decades of the second century, the Eucharist or Lord's Supper included *an actual supper*—with thanksgiving over bread at the beginning, then the meal, with the thanksgiving over wine cup at the end. It may be difficult for contemporary Christians who have adequate or more than adequate food and drink to imagine how significant sharing a meal might be to those ancient and contemporary persons struggling with poverty, wondering if there will be any food tomorrow.[7]

---

row. Why pews? Worshipers found it difficult to stand for lengthy sermons. Roman Catholics began to adopt Protestant practice by including pews or chairs in churches.

[7] Recall that in the United States, a sizable percentage of the population struggles with poverty, as evidenced in the numerous religious and humanitarian organizations that feed hungry people every day in addition to supplying produce for food banks, meal sites, and hungry children programs throughout the entire year.

"Christian cells met together within *insulae* (shop apartments) with mutual rather than patronal support. Each brought what he or she could to the common meal, and thus all were assured, no matter what happened, of at least one Eucharist—*one thankworthy meal*—per week."[8] In this meal practice, there was sufficient food and drink for all—provided that each person was conscious of all others who were being fed from the one table. Thus, a participant needed to limit his or her consumption so that other meal participants would have enough to eat. Does this practice not sound similar to the wilderness experience when manna was collected sufficient for one's daily needs? Of course the God of Israel was the generous Provider of nourishment—the patron, as it were, of the Hebrews—but this just distribution was incumbent on people recognizing limitations, on restrained eating so that others might be fed as well. It goes without saying that restraint, that recognizing and accepting limitations, is not currently a well-practiced American virtue.[9]

To be sure, the early Christian communal share meal was an economic system *in micro*, a way of managing or caring for the household that assured all participants of food and drink regardless of physical ability, economic status, gender, race, or ethnicity—an assurance grounded in the practice

---

[8] Crossan, *The Birth of Christianity*, 429; emphasis mine.

[9] "Economic growth" without limitations is the refrain chanted by politicians, economists, and business leaders in neoliberal economies that have emerged since the end of the Second World War. As Pope Francis has argued, the notion of constant expansion and unlimited growth has become a reckless ideology, a global "religion," that continues to serve the interests of the wealthiest persons and corporations within the wealthiest nations at the expense of the poor and destitute in the poorest nations—an ideology that continues to wreak havoc on the environment.

of Jesus of Nazareth: "You give them something to eat."[10] Indeed, the sharing of food and drink among all present at the communal meal, regardless of status, was a sign of Christ's presence among them. Why? In a world where discrimination, inequity, and destitution were considered normal and experienced by the majority of the population, the communal share meal was perceived as nothing less than miraculous, the in-breaking of heaven on earth, an unexpected manifestation of what Jesus preached: "the kingdom of God is in your midst." In this meal practice, mutual care among the participants mitigated dependency upon an earthly patron: "All eyes look to you, O God, and you give them their food in due season . . . You open wide your hand and feed every living thing." One wonders: did they recognize in the sharing of food and drink across social boundaries—a practice *unheard of* in their society—the real presence of Christ, *real* because this countercultural practice of mutual care stood in stark contrast to cultural norms? Did they recognize in this practice the One who had directed the distribution of bread and fish to all in need in a deserted place?

The patronal meal continues in the world today; after all, children, the homebound infirm, persons in hospitals and nursing homes, the incarcerated, individuals with severe mental challenges, the destitute, and military recruits—to name only a few—are dependent on others for their daily bread. One wonders, however, if the common share meal— the potluck—will survive. Does the contemporary American practice of purchasing ready-made food for oneself or one's

---

[10] Nor should we overlook the radical act of Christian baptism in which those factors that would divide people from one another in the dominant society were critiqued and "washed away" in the stream or font: race and ethnicity (Jew and Greek), gender (male and female), and economic status (slave and free); see Galatians 3:27-28.

household, of eating alone, on the run, or while competing with technological distractions make a shared meal an anachronism?[11] And if a meal is shared in the home, does everyone obtain food from one dish, thus ensuring that participants become mindful of others who will be eating from the one dish, an invitation to practice a measure of restraint so that others might have sufficient? And what of the communal share meal in the church? Christian practice, with a few exceptions, has followed the ritual pattern that emerged in the second century: thanksgiving over bread and wine leading to eating and drinking. As one scholar notes, Christians now receive a sip of wine and a taste of bread symbolic of a real meal that no longer exists. What would happen, he asks, if they kept a real meal symbolic of Jesus's actual meal practice?[12]

What has not been forgotten entirely is the early Christian practice of each worshiper bringing some bread, some wine, and some food to the Sunday liturgy, with an appropriate amount of bread and wine brought to the altar for the Eucharist, the rest set aside and then distributed at the end of the liturgy to those in need of food and drink. Members of

---

[11] While earlier generations of Americans experienced the practice of sharing from one common dish or dishes at a meal, consider the pervasive practice in fast-food chains of selling individualized meals and the growing practice in grocery stores of marketing prepackaged meals suitable for one customer. The practice in some Christian communions of using individual wafers and individual shot glasses filled with wine prior to their consecration reflect and thus complement the highly individualized marketing techniques of the food industry in North America. Such eucharistic practice makes it extremely difficult to preach and teach the Pauline insight concerning the unity of the Body of Christ fed with the one Bread and one Cup of the Eucharist. One can repeatedly sing the words, "One bread, one Body, one Lord of all," but the actual practice of offering individual hosts or cubes of precut bread contradicts the words spoken or sung.

[12] Crossan, *The Birth of Christianity*, 424.

the assembly thus received a portion of bread as the Body of Christ while the remaining bread was offered to those in need. What if such a practice were to prevail in the churches today: Might the assembly come to grasp the intrinsic relationship between the self-giving of Christ in the Eucharist and the generous offering of food and drink to one's hungry neighbors? In this regard, the deacon has played a significant role as the one who ministers the eucharistic cup and then leads in the distribution of food and drink to the hungry poor.[13] Or this: food and drink, brought by members of the assembly on Sunday, become a "farmer's market" on Friday, a food distribution site arranged around the altar for those who struggle with limited or no income, thus underscoring the economic dimension of the Eucharist.[14] Or this: from the food and drink presented at the Eucharist, members of the assembly participate in preparing, serving, and sharing a meal after the Sunday liturgy with the homeless and hungry poor, participating in and providing "at least *one thankworthy meal* during the week."[15] But, then, one

---

[13] See Ambrose of Milan, *De Officiis: Introduction, Text, and Translation*, ed. Ivor Davidson (Oxford: Oxford University Press, 2001), on the diaconal ministry and martyrdom of St. Lawrence of Rome, who, according to the remarkable legends of his life, recognized the intrinsic relationship between ministering the eucharistic cup and ministering among and with the poor.

[14] See Sara Miles, *Jesus Freak: Feeding, Healing, Raising the Dead* (San Francisco: Jossey-Bass, 2010), and the Food Pantry she established at St. Gregory of Nyssa Church, http://www.saintgregorys.org/the-food -pantry.html, in which food for those in need is arranged around the free-standing altar. To be sure, this is not a common share meal but it does make visible the relationship between the free distribution of Sunday's eucharistic bread and wine and the free distribution of Friday's food and drink. It also serves as a visible criticism of the wealthiest nation in human history: a nation unable or unwilling to respond to the most basic need of all its citizens through the agency of its government.

[15] Note the difference between *serving* a meal to people who are hungry and *sharing* a meal with those who are hungry. In the former, there may

wonders if those who struggle with poverty and chronic hunger are present in the churches.

Troubling Questions

These various efforts participate in the work of Christian charity, of faith active in love, of sharing one's surplus with those in need. Such charitable work has been inspired among many Christians by a Matthean parable: "The king will say to those at his right hand, 'Come, you that are blessed by my Father, inherit the kingdom prepared for you from the foundation of the world; for I was hungry and you gave me food, I was thirsty and you gave me something to drink, I was a stranger and you welcomed me, I was naked and you gave me clothing, I was sick and you took care of me, I was in prison and you visited me.' "[16] Others point to the apostle Paul, who promoted a collection among the churches of Asia Minor to support Jerusalem Christ followers who were suffering in the midst of famine.[17] Today, the social assistance provided by the churches participates in the larger "food relief industry" that emerged during the

---

be little contact between servers and guests—a practice that resembles a school cafeteria buffet. In the latter, the meal is served from common dishes at each table; servers and guests eat and converse with each other at table and thus share both food and life. In the latter, the chance of knowing one another as human beings and engendering friendships increases, overcoming the division created in the former practice. See *The Fatted Calf Café* at http://fattedcalfcafe.org and the *Sant'Egidio Christmas Lunch* at http://www.santegidio.org/pageID/35/langID/en/The -Christmas-Lunch.html.

[16] Matthew 25:34-36; see Matthew 25:31-46 (LM: Ord 34A or CKing A; ELW: L 34A, NewY ABC; RCL: NewY ABC, Pr. 29 A).

[17] See Acts 24:17; Galatians 2:1-10; 2 Corinthians 8–9, and then, 2 Corinthians 8:7, 9, 13-15 (LM: Ord 13B); 2 Corinthians 8:7-15 (ELW: L 13B; RCL: Pr. 8B).

1960s.[18] Such charity responds to immediate need; it provides nourishment for one day, one week, or one month for homeless persons, the elderly on limited incomes, single mothers, and children whose parents must work two or three jobs to provide housing and some but not sufficient food throughout the month.[19]

At the same time, any charitable response to immediate need rightly leads one to ask, *why is charity needed in the first place?* In one of the wealthiest nations in human history, why do millions of people continue to suffer with food insecurity? Why do so many people still go hungry at the "feast" of American life promised to immigrants? Why has the phenomenal growth of charitable giving for the hungry poor failed to secure a lasting solution to this chronic outrage in national life? Is it possible that many Christians are simply content to "remember the poor" and "take up a collection" from their surplus—to offer a handout—but cannot imagine that they, together with many other Christians, could change their patterns of consumption—accept limitations—and thus provoke a wider questioning of an economy driven by overconsumption? Other than religious orders of strict observance, does anyone seek to live a *downwardly* mobile life?

---

[18] See *A Place at the Table*, ed. Peter Pringle (Philadelphia: Perseus Books/Public Affairs, 2013); see also the earlier work by Loretta Schwartz-Nobel on the resiliency of food insecurity in the United States and her analysis of the wild swings between government-sponsored attempts to *penalize* the hungry poor or *serve* the hungry poor: *Growing Up Empty: The Hunger Epidemic in America* (New York: Harper, 2001).

[19] Limited income will go first to housing expenses—who wants to live on the street, especially with children?—and then to food and drink, medicine and toiletries. But when there is insufficient income to purchase food, households eat less or parents refrain from eating in order to ensure that children have some food. Food banks and meal sites participate in the "safety net" that sustains individuals and households.

Or is it this: That the supporters of an economic system devoted to the unregulated acquisition of capital for the individual and the corporation recognize no limitations whatsoever, no equitable sharing, no restraint so that others might simply live? Is it possible that the current economic system cannot be questioned because many Christian institutions—parishes, schools, charities, universities, hospitals, social agencies, clergy pensions, religious orders, investment funds—benefit from a system that tolerates giving from one's surplus yet is resistant, utterly resistant, to any serious reform that would seriously diminish hunger and poverty?[20] One is reminded of the controversial words of Hélder Câmara, archbishop of Olinda and Recife in Brazil: "When I give food to the poor, they call me a saint. When I ask *why* they are poor, they call me a communist."[21]

In the practice of the Eucharist, each person—regardless of gender, orientation, age, race, ethnicity, and economic status—receives the same amount of food and drink. The Hispanic minister of the chalice receives no more wine than the African American bank executive and the white factory worker. The single priest or married pastor receives the same amount of bread as the straight high school student and the lesbian librarian. The presider, in breaking apart

[20] Consider the 2013 UNICEF study of the thirty-five most developed nations in the world. Finland's mixed economic system (capitalist and socialist) supports the nation's top commitment: the well-being of all citizens in food, housing, education, healthcare, childcare, eldercare, and job training. Less than 5 percent of all Finnish children live in poverty. While Finland is ranked first in citizen well-being and citizen happiness (along with Denmark, Iceland, Norway, and Sweden), the United States is ranked thirty-fourth in child poverty and other indicators that sustain high levels of poverty and hunger; only Romania is ranked below the US at thirty-five.

[21] Zildo Rocha, *Helder the Gift: A Life That Marked the Course of the Church in Brazil*, trans. unknown (Petropolis: Editora Vozes, 2000), 53.

the loaf of bread, must ensure that there are sufficient fragments for all who come with hands open to receive. Those who sip from the chalice need to be mindful of others who will drink from the cup: not drinking too little, not drinking too much. Does this practice enter the preaching and teaching that rightly open up the meaning of what many may take for granted? Are worshiping assemblies aware that the practice of limitation and restraint constitutes part of their formation in an ethical Eucharist?

This eucharistic practice is nothing less than a *sacramental economy* that stands in sharp contrast to the inequity and predatory ethos of the current economic system that rules the lives of many. Is it possible, then, that this economy of grace, celebrated in thousands of churches throughout the land, offers participants a way to consider how an economy ought to serve human and ecological flourishing? What did the American Catholic bishops teach regarding *any* economic system? "The economy exists for the person, not the person for the economy. . . . Economic choices and institutions must be judged by how they protect or undermine the life and dignity of the human person and serve the common good. All people have a right to life and to secure the basic necessities of life."[22] Such principles lead one into the challenging work of seeking economic justice, of asking, "Why are they hungry?"

"The whole group of those who believed were of one heart and soul, and no one claimed private ownership of any possessions, but everything they owned was held in common. . . . There was not a needy person among them, for as many as owned lands or houses sold them and brought the proceeds of what was sold. They laid it at the apostles' feet, and it was distributed to each as any had

[22] http://www.usccb.org/issues-and-action/human-life-and-dignity /economic-justice-economy/catholic-framework-for-economic-life.cfm.

need."[23] Unbelievable, isn't it? Indeed, a good many contemporary biblical scholars have dismissed this account as nothing more than a Lucan fantasy. And yet this economy of generous sharing, flowing from the breaking of the bread, has prompted continued reform in church and society—a reform advanced in the sermons, writings, and practice of the early church fathers,[24] the Rule of St. Benedict,[25] the Primitive Rule and practice of St. Francis,[26] Luther's writings and early church orders,[27] the communitarian experiments of the Hutterites[28] and the Shakers,[29] the Jesuit socialist *reducciones* in Latin America,[30] John Wesley's com-

---

[23] Acts 4:32, 34-35; see Acts 4:32-37 (LM, ELW, RCL: East 2B).

[24] See *St. Basil the Great: On Social Justice*, trans. C. Paul Schroeder (Crestwood, NY: St. Vladimir Seminary Press, 2009); Susan Holman, *The Hungry Are Dying: Beggars and Bishops in Roman Cappadocia* (New York: Oxford University Press, 2001); Peter Phan, *Social Thought: Message of the Fathers of the Church* (Wilmington: Michael Glazier, 1983).

[25] See the commentary on chapters 33 ("Whether the monks should consider anything their own") and 34 ("Whether all should receive necessities in equal measure") in Kardong, *Benedict's Rule*, 272–288.

[26] See *Francis of Assisi—The Saint: Early Documents*, vol. 1, ed. Regis Armstrong, OFMCap. (Hyde Park: New City Press, 1999); *Franciscans and Preaching: Every Miracle from the Beginning of the World Came about through Words*, ed. Timothy Johnson (Leiden: Brill, 2012).

[27] See Martin Luther, "The Blessed Sacrament of the Holy and True Body of Christ, and the Brotherhoods" and "Preface to the Ordinance of a Common Chest," in *Luther's Works* 35 and 45 (Philadelphia: Fortress Press, 1960; 1962); Samuel Torvend, *Luther and the Hungry Poor: Gathered Fragments* (Minneapolis: Fortress Press, 2008).

[28] See Werner Packull, *Hutterite Beginnings: Communitarian Experiments during the Reformation*, rev. ed. (Baltimore: Johns Hopkins University Press, 1999).

[29] See Stephen Stein, *The Shaker Experience in America: A History of the United Society of Believers* (New Haven: Yale University Press, 1994).

[30] See Walter Nonneman, "On the Economics of the Socialist Theocracy of the Jesuits in Paraguay, 1609–1767, " in *The Political Economy of Theocracy*, ed. Mario Ferrero and Ronald Wintrobe (New York: Palgrave

mitment to the hungry poor,[31] promoters of the Social Gospel,[32] Anglo-Catholic preaching on the Mass and socialism,[33] the pioneering work of Virgil Michel, OSB, on liturgy and capitalism,[34] the ministry of Dorothy Day and the Catholic Worker Movement,[35] and the social teaching of the magisterium.[36] In all this, the historian hears many voices that give witness throughout the centuries to an ethical Eucharist. "As love and support are given to you in the sacrament of the altar, you in turn must render love and support to Christ in his needy ones. You must feel with sorrow . . . all the unjust suffering of the innocent with which the world is everywhere filled to overflowing. You must fight, work, and pray."[37] And this, too: "The prayer

---

Macmillan, 2009), 119–142; Philip Caraman, *The Lost Paradise: The Jesuit Republic in South America* (London: Sidgwick & Jackson, 1975).

[31] See Theodore Jennings, Jr., *Good News to the Poor: John Wesley's Evangelical Economics* (Nashville: Abingdon Press, 1990).

[32] See Christopher Evans, *The Social Gospel in American Religion: A History* (New York: New York University Press, 2017); Walter Rauschenbusch, *Christianity and the Social Crisis* (Louisville: Westminster John Knox, 1994).

[33] See John Orens, *Stewart Headlam's Radical Anglicanism: The Mass, the Masses, and the Music Hall* (Urbana: University of Illinois Press, 2003).

[34] See Virgil Michel, OSB, *The Social Question: Essays on Capitalism and Christianity* (Collegeville: Saint John's University, 1987).

[35] See Thomas Loome, "The Real Presence(s) of Christ in the Life and Thought of Dorothy Day, Key to Her Canonization," in *The Houston Worker* (August 23, 2013), at http://cjd.org/2013/08/23/the-real-presences-of-christ-in-the-life-and-thought-of-dorothy-day-key-to-her-canonization/; on the relationship between Virgil Michel, OSB, and Dorothy Day, see Mark Zwick and Louise Zwick, *The Catholic Worker Movement: Intellectual and Spiritual Origins* (New York: Paulist Press, 2005), 58–74.

[36] See *Catholic Social Thought: The Documentary Heritage*, ed. David O'Brien and Thomas Shannon (Maryknoll: Orbis Books, 2010); *Modern Catholic Social Teaching: Commentaries and Interpretations*, ed. Kenneth Himes (Washington, DC: Georgetown University Press, 2005).

[37] Luther, LW 35:54.

which we repeat at every Mass, 'Give us this day our daily bread,' obliges us to do everything possible to end the scandal of hunger. Formed in the school of the Eucharist, Christians are called to assume their political and social responsibilities."[38]

Formation of Conscience

In many churches, those who eat and drink at the Eucharist rightly say "Amen" as bread and wine are offered to them. And even if no such word of assent is uttered, the very act of eating and drinking is, in truth, an assent to the reception of this bread and this wine. Yet such assent, through word or act, is not only the recognition that bread and wine are given to the communicant, not only a recognition that this bread fragment is the Body of the Christ, this sip of wine his Blood, but also one's assent to this uncommon practice, to the generous sharing of food and drink that extends to those who are hungry and thirsty regardless of their status in society. It is an assent to and reception of the *practice* that begins with and extends beyond the Supper. One wonders if the people of God recognize that their reception of the sacrament—their reception of this sacramental economy—commits them to its promotion in the world.

For Catholics and other Christians who reflect on the meaning of this central Christian action, the temptation is ever present to "explain" the mystery of the Eucharist and thus reduce its "richness" to one thing—yet one rarely finds inspiration in explanations. The temptation that faces the catechist, teacher, and preacher is to engage in moralistic discourse, telling people what they must do—and if they don't, what will happen to them. The temptation that faces

---

[38] Benedict XVI, *Sacramentum Caritatis* 91.

all Christians is to "spiritualize" the Eucharist into "other-worldliness"—and thus avoid the earthly reality that without food and drink, there is only death.[39] In one of his sermons preached during the fifth century, Leo I set forth the relationship between Jesus of Nazareth and the Christian community in this manner: "The actions (*sacramenta*) of the Redeemer during his life on earth have passed into the life of his Body in the actions (*sacramenta*) of the church."[40] To focus, then, on the *sacramentum* leads one to the meal practice of Jesus and his followers—a practice rooted in the biblical images of God's generous feeding of all creation, as these stories, present in the Lectionary, give shape to an ethic formed in eucharistic practice. Might such reflection on the invitations to follow the worldly trajectory of the Eucharist, the Mass, provoke new insight and animate communal action?

This is to suggest that sacramental practice sets forth a social ethic marked by a commitment to social justice.[41] This does not discard classic expressions of eucharistic meaning—sacrifice, remembrance, forgiveness—but in light of

[39] See Samuel Torvend, "Proclaiming and Preaching," in *Ordo: Bath, World, Prayer, Table: A Liturgical Primer in Honor of Gordon W. Lathrop*, ed. Dirk Lange and Dwight Vogel (Akron: OSL Publications, 2005), 58–70.

[40] Leo I, *St. Leo the Great: Sermons*, in *Fathers of the Church* 93, trans. Jane Freeland and Agnes Conway (Washington, DC: Catholic University of America Press, 1996), 326.

[41] See James Empereur, SJ and Christopher Kiesling, OP, *The Liturgy That Does Justice* (Collegeville: Liturgical Press, 1990), with their comprehensive examination of the Lectionary and sacraments. Consider, also, this series of texts: *Liturgy and Social Justice*, ed. Mark Searle (Collegeville: Liturgical Press, 1980); *Living No Longer for Ourselves: Liturgy and Justice in the Nineties*, ed. Kathleen Hughes, RSCJ, and Mark Francis, CSV (Collegeville: Liturgical Press, 1991); Paul Westermeyer, *Let Justice Sing: Hymnody and Justice* (Collegeville: Liturgical Press, 1998); and *Liturgy and Justice: To Worship God in Spirit and Truth* (Collegeville: Liturgical Press, 2002).

the symbolic richness of all liturgical and sacramental practice, the promotion of social justice cannot be overlooked. And what is social justice but the public form of Christian love for others, for one's neighbor, especially those who suffer injustice by virtue of gender, orientation, race, ethnicity, socioeconomic and educational status. While "morality" or "ethics" are often cast as obedience to law, as discerning right and wrong behaviors, another view suggests that Christian ethics draws one to a person—Jesus Christ—and asks what it means to live as one of his disciples in the world today.[42] The suggestion offered here is that *eucharistic practice, animated by the practice of Jesus and his many followers over 2,000 years, sets forth a social and ethical vision*, a vision into which Christian assemblies can lean into and live. Thus, we ask the question: Will this central ritual practice—the Mass, the Holy Eucharist—be received as a lively and life-giving ethical vision in the assemblies of the churches today?

> The epistles and gospels were written to convey memories about Jesus from those who had known him before his death to those who wanted to know him afterward. But in addition to memories, these texts were written to convey instructions for recognizing the Lord in real time, that is, *for finding Jesus incognito in our present circumstances*. Of course memories are easier to accept than instructions, because memories refer back to a past time; what they recall is presumed to be settled and closed. Thus it is relatively easy . . . to take up bread and cup in remembrance of the fact that Jesus lived here once upon a time. It is much less easy to seek Jesus in the present, even though we know where he is dwelling. It is difficult to worship in expectation of responding to the invitations he gives us right now in the needs of the hungry, the thirsty, and the homeless

---

[42] See the remarkable work by David Cunningham, *Christian Ethics: The End of the Law* (London and New York: Routledge, 2008), 12, in which the author draws on Christian liturgy as the primary source of Christian ethics.

(Matthew 25:31-40). Their pleas for help are coming to us from
Jesus . . . incognito.[43]

We may say many things of this ecclesial action that some
early Christians called the breaking of the bread. After all,
we have pointed to the "inexhaustible riches" of a sacramental action that cannot be reduced to one thing; the Scriptures, the liturgy, and the Christian tradition all witness
against such minimalistic instincts. At the same time, we
have noted that eucharistic practice is not only an act of
thanksgiving, a spiritual sacrifice, a memorial of the Lord's
passion, an act of forgiveness, or intimate union with Christ,
but also this: an ethical practice that expands outward into
the world, offering life in the midst of diminishment and
death.

And so we ask, having encountered the prophet of Nazareth in bread and wine cup, will the assembly be alert to the
invitations that are coming from him today? For he is there:
present among those who suffer with hunger, with people
marginalized by culture and religion, in this earth that cries
out for healing, among the many who yearn to dwell in the
economy of grace, and those who struggle with poverty,
who have but one prayer that rests at the heart of the Mass:
"Give us this day our daily bread." The prophet of the Galilee is the wounded and risen One who offers this invitation
to his followers: You give them something to eat. One only
wonders if Christians will have the courage to do so.

[43] Marianne Sawicki, "How Can Worship Be Contemporary?," in *What
Is Contemporary Worship?*, ed. Gordon Lathrop (Minneapolis: Augsburg
Fortress, 1995), 29, emphasis mine. See also her *Seeing the Lord: Resurrec-
tion and Early Christian Practice* (Minneapolis: Fortress Press, 1994).

Chapter Seven

Eucharistic Limitations

The Privileges of the Leisure Class

In 1899, Thorstein Veblen, a Norwegian American economist, published *The Theory of the Leisure Class: An Economic Study of Institutions*,[1] a landmark study of American culture and its economic system. In his work, Veblen argued that as industrial manufacturing—industrialism—became a dominant force in North America, the production of goods met the material needs of a society growing rapidly through immigration and high birth rates. But more than meeting the material needs of society, the production of goods reaped astounding profits for those who controlled the means of production: the owners of factories and plants whose assembly lines churned out a multitude of products—from steel to cloth to chemicals. The enormous wealth held by the owners, argued Veblen, prompted the public display of such wealth in what he called "conspicuous consumption," what others have called the cult of materialism. The new-found wealth derived from industrialism was not to be hidden in bank vaults or behind gated estates and so diminish the possibility of envy, theft, or competition for even more. Rather, in the "gilded age," such wealth was pre-

[1] Macmillan in New York first published Veblen's work in 1899. Oxford University Press republished it in 2009 as an Oxford World Classic text.

sented in the most ostentatious and public means possible.[2] This glittering display of material prosperity thus entered quickly into the mythology of American life and sounded like this: a diligent and efficient work ethic, with a bit of luck or the aid of divine providence, could eventually produce wealth for even the poorest immigrant. Veblen, however, demurred from such an optimistic view of wealth display and considered it the survival of a "predatory" instinct from the early history of human development: wealth display serves to humiliate and shame those who do not possess wealth and creates a corrosive class consciousness fraught with moral assumptions.[3]

At the same time, the industrial revolution and its capacity for the mass production of goods—from automobiles and cutlery to books and clothing—encouraged the purchase of such goods in growing numbers: what had once been sold at prohibitive cost to the few was now available at much lower prices to the many. And yet, mass production and its hoped-for twin, mass consumption, led to a crisis in the first decades of the twentieth century—an *overproduction* of goods that far outstripped demand. How could this crisis of too many manufactured goods, sitting unsold in a warehouse,

---

[2] Veblen claimed that the subjugation of women was an example of conspicuous consumption: the wife who did not need to work could be "displayed" by her husband as a testament to his hard work and his wealth. Religious devotions, he argued at the end of the nineteenth century, are another example of such consumption: the leisure class has the wealth to build and endow churches that serve no "useful" function in society, such as the amelioration of social ills. The same can be said of professional sports, he argued: the leisure class can spend considerable wealth on athletic competitions that also serve no useful function in society other than to entertain those who have the time and leisure to pay for such entertainments while the "lower" classes must labor just to make ends meet.

[3] "Upper class" connoting a "higher" moral order; "lower class" suggesting an "inferior" moral order.

be resolved if one were the owner of a factory or plant? After all, the primary goal was, and remains, the accrual of profit for those who control the means of production and their shareholders: no sale, no profit. Consequently, manufacturers began to employ, and continue to employ, two strategies: planned obsolescence—the planned deterioration or decreasing "usefulness" of products over time—and the use of carefully planned advertising to create in the minds of the public a need for a new version of the older product, a need that could only be met by purchasing the product and thus increasing consumer spending. In effect, the use of planned obsolescence and persuasive advertising produced an ideology that normalized increasing mass consumption, an ideology that has taken hold in the American soul despite periodic slumps in the economy. Acquiring more, it would seem, is the better goal. Indeed, who would want to be viewed as out of style or old fashioned by neglecting to buy ever-new iterations of the same product that promises the allure of being up to date and "contemporary"? Let us be clear: it is this pervasive "consumer" ideology that cannot abide the thought of limitations, of living with less rather than more and more.[4] One then wonders: Has the normalization of a consuming society effectively shaped the souls of Christians and their leaders?[5]

---

[4] Veblen argued that the practice of conspicuous consumption by the wealthy and the pursuit of material gain by workers built upon the stratification of society first recognized in medieval trade capitalism and early modern global mercantile capitalism. The pursuit of wealth thus carried strong individualistic overtones: wealth accrual for the individual (and his or her family), or for the individual owner of the company, or for the individual shareholder in the company who benefited from the profit realized in sales. Robber baron philanthropy, applauded by the news media (media owned by the "barons"), distracted attention from the depressing conditions in which workers labored.

[5] Perhaps it has been this way in the US for decades if not longer—the quantification of spiritual life as witnessed in an obsession with statistics:

Prophetic Fasting

One way in which Christians have expressed skepticism of a cultural mandate to acquire more and more is the practice of fasting, of setting a limitation on the consumption of food—food as symbol for all material goods. In an overconsuming culture, fasting is the refusal to consume more than one actually needs.[6] The juxtaposition of the "spiritual" practice of fasting with a culture conditioned to "material" acquisitiveness may seem odd at first, especially if one has been raised with the notion that fasting is a form of penance or repentance for one's failings toward God and toward others. It may sound odd if one has been taught that "giving up" something for a period of time pleases God (for then one would have to wrestle with the possibility that giving up more and more pleases God more and more, and where would that lead?). And it may sound odd if one assumes that fasting is a form of self-discipline little different from losing weight or training for a race. Many Christians are familiar with the fast as a spiritual practice that prepares the individual or community for something else: keeping a solemnity or holy day (such as the Easter Vigil), receiving baptism, professing solemn vows in a religious order, or being ordained to public ministry.[7] To fast, say some, is to

---

average Sunday attendance; budget size; staff positions; annual reports for the diocese or synod that ask for little more than numbers. It would seem that the quantity of number seems to trump quality of life.

[6] The "simple living" or "simplicity" movement promotes voluntary practices that influence eating habits, food sustainability, shelter, clothing, and work location. This movement, with many adherents drawn from the middle class, should be distinguished from the experience of systemic poverty.

[7] One wonders, however, if the prebaptismal fast is actually known and practiced and if candidates for ordination or solemn vows recognize prayer and fasting as a worthwhile entrance into public ministry or lifelong commitment to a religious order. The practice was diminished

imitate Jesus in his wilderness fast (Luke 4:2; Matt 4:2)[8] or to follow his instruction to "put oil on your head and wash your face, so that your fasting may be seen not by others but by your Father who is in secret" (Matt 6:17-18).[9] Here we recognize the significance of the various spiritual motives for fasting in the Christian tradition. At the same time, recent historical research invites us to consider other dimensions of this ancient and global practice.

Scholars of the Mediterranean cultural context in which Jesus and his ancestors lived suggest that refraining from eating and drinking was intended to communicate *affliction* to one's community and thus elicit a response from those who witnessed the debilitating nature of the fast.[10] Refusing food and drink thus served as a form of protest in the presence of evil. If anything, fasting was a form of lament, of heartfelt anguish, of crying out in pain. Rejecting food and drink, inattention to one's looks, and lack of concern for one's clothing could be expressed in deteriorating health, placing ashes on one's face or head, and wearing sackcloth or degraded clothing. These responses to affliction—prompted by the death or killing of a family member or the loss of one's land, labor, or health—begged one's friends to do something: to join in one's mourning or to seek and bring

---

or abolished by a number of sixteenth-century reforming groups who came to be called Protestant. Eastern Orthodox Christians, Roman Catholics, and Anglicans keep a fast on Ash Wednesday, Good Friday, and other fast days. Despite Luther and Calvin's hesitancy regarding the practice, Lutherans and Presbyterians may be encouraged to fast but are not required to do so. The same holds for Methodists, some Baptist groups, and Quakers.

[8] Luke 4:1-13 (LM: Epi 3C; LM, ELW, RCL: Lent 1C) and Matthew 4:1-11 (LM, ELW, RCL: Lent 1A).

[9] LM, ELW, RCL: AshW ABC.

[10] Bruce Malina and Richard Rohrbaugh, *Social Scientific Commentary on the Gospels*, 2nd ed. (Minneapolis: Fortress Press, 2003), 360.

to justice the perpetrator of murder or the agent of one's misery. The wearing of sackcloth—coarse material fashioned from the hair of a black goat—is one instance in the long history of donning clothing in various colors to express mourning, dissent, or a call to action.[11] Placing ashes on one's head or refusing to wash one's face or body demonstrated desolation or ruin. Not so much giving up something "for God" or doing penance for one's failings, fasting was the immediate response to distress and misfortune.

Fasting also acknowledged *economic or political disaster*. Perhaps the primal text that exemplifies this dimension of fasting is Isaiah 58:1-12, a reading proclaimed in the churches during winter Ordinary Time (the Epiphany season) and on Ash Wednesday.[12] Having returned from exile in Babylon, the people of God wonder why their prayer and their fast find no pleasing response from their divine Liberator and Provider:

> "Why do we fast, but you do not see? Why humble ourselves, but you do not notice?" Look, you serve your own interest on your fast day, and oppress all your workers. Look, you fast only to quarrel and to fight and to strike with a wicked fist. Such fasting as you do today will not make your voice heard on high.

---

[11] One is mindful of the use of the tricolor in protest of the extravagances of the French monarchy and its absolutist claims in the eighteenth century; of nineteenth-century American women wearing white clothing as a form of protest and mourning in the suffrage movement; of twentieth-century protestors in the United Farm Workers movement donning shirts imprinted with an image of Our Lady of Guadalupe; of twenty-first-century protesters at G8 Summits wearing black clothing from head to toe.

[12] LM: Ord 5A; ELW: L 5A, Ash ABC, L 21C; RCL: Epi 5A, Ash ABC, Pr. 16C. See also Joshua 7:1-10 (Israelite overconfidence leads to disaster and resultant fasting) and Judges 20:24-28 (weeping and fasting due to defeat)—in both instances, fasting takes place in presence of the Ark of the Covenant, the center of worship.

Is such the fast that I choose, a day to humble oneself? Is it to bow down the head like a bulrush, and to lie in sackcloth and ashes? Will you call this a fast, a day acceptable to the Lord? Is not this the fast that I choose: to loose the bonds of injustice, to undo the thongs of the yoke, to let the oppressed go free, and to break every yoke? Is it not to share your bread with the hungry, and bring the homeless poor into your house; when you see the naked, to cover them, and not to hide yourself from your own kin? (Isaiah 58:3-7)[13]

Is fasting rejected in this condemnation of social injustice, of breaking the social responsibilities of the Covenant? No. Rather, the prophet claims that the practice of fasting—a regular part of Second Temple devotion—becomes meaning-ful, "acceptable," when manifested in acts of justice for the oppressed, in attending to basic human need by ensuring an equitable distribution of bread, caring for the homeless, clothing the naked, and offering hospitality to strangers. In other words, the "spiritual" practice bears within it an eco-nomic and social meaning, a liberating and life-giving meaning that is directed not to the self but to others in need. What the prophet witnesses in the faith community, how-ever, are contempt for the poor, injustice, and a perversion of the laws that benefits the leisure class alone. He thus calls the comfortable to a fast oriented toward those who suffer, for "to fast and neglect the poor perverts religion."[14] Do we not hear an echo of the Isaiah text in Matthew's parable of the last judgment (25:31-46) and Luke's account of Jesus's

---

[13] See also Amos 4 (prophetic condemnation of conspicuous consump-tion) and 5:18-27 (prophetic condemnation of a corrupted legal system that favors wealthy elites). As noted earlier, Amos 4 is not included in LM, ELW, and RCL. Amos 5 is not included in LM Sunday and Solemnity readings but in the Thirteenth Week of the Year; for Amos 5:6-15 (ELW: L 28B; RCL: Pr. 23B) and Amos 5:18-24 (ELW: L 32A; RCL: Pr. 27A).

[14] NJBC 21:54.

mission to bring good news to the poor, release to captives, and freedom to the oppressed (4:14-21)?

What, then, of Jesus's fast in the wilderness, a story proclaimed at the beginning of the season of Lent? How many times have lyrics, prayers, and homilies suggested that the story is about one thing: as Jesus was tempted, so, too, is the Christian—and thus, Lent invites the individual to struggle with those temptations that distract from faith in God? But is the sole meaning of the episode personal? Consider, then, the framework of the story: the forty days and nights Jesus spends in the wilderness—the inspiration for the forty days of Lent. Note that the number forty is found in the flood narrative of Genesis wherein God observes *violence and corruption in society* and recreates human community through flooding waters. Note that another use of the number is the forty years during which the Hebrews traveled out of *a society marked by the conspicuous display of imperial wealth, authoritarian corruption, and economic enslavement*,[15] and entered into a new way of living with one another under the guidance of their divine Liberator, the One who provided adequate food and drink for every woman, child, and man.[16] Note yet another use of the number: the forty days after which Nineveh would be destroyed for its *collective wickedness* unless it heeded the preaching of Jonah. In each instance, fasting and forty are linked to a *social crisis*. And thus, for Jesus, living in a society marked by chronic food shortages that often arose from elite control

---

[15] The gospel writers—Matthew in particular—invoke the memory of the forty-year postexodus journey in the wilderness during which the Hebrews experienced hunger and grumbled against God. By way of contrast, Jesus, as the "head" of a newly emerging humanity, also experiences hunger but demonstrates his trust in God, no grumbling, by refusing to accept the challenge of the Tempter to transform stone into bread.

[16] This is a reference to the distribution of manna such that each household enjoyed sufficient for each day: not too little and not too much.

of agriculture, his fast not only communicates absolute loyalty to his father, the God of Israel, but also solidarity with those in his society, and every society, who must contend with inadequate food and drink ("Turn these stones into bread"), authoritarian corruption ("All these I will give you, if you will fall down and worship me"), and violence as a tool of social control ("If you are the Son of God, throw yourself down"). In their narration of Jesus's fasting and temptation, the evangelists are keen to present *in micro* the good news of the kingdom of God: wherever Jesus is there is absolute dependence on God and what God offers to humankind: benevolent care, peace, and adequate nourishment—not just for the few but for the many.

Here, then, is the marvelous juxtaposition: the One who fasts throughout forty days will provide God's gift of food and drink for the many. Fasting—limitation—is set next to feasting—abundance.

Yes, the fast of forty days can be a spiritual practice that focuses one's loyalty or faith in God and God alone. And yet, there is no generic God.[17] Christians claim that the immortal and invisible God is revealed in Jesus of Nazareth, son of Mary, and that this Jesus was oriented toward others who lived in a particular society marked by little mercy and many injustices. Is it possible, then, to recognize his fast and his counsel to keep a fast as a self-imposed limitation in a society marked by incredible inequities and discriminations—sinful attitudes and practices—at odds with his vision of shared, peaceful, and compassionate life in the kingdom of God? Perhaps his Christian followers fail to remember that fasting is inextricably linked to sharing un-

---

[17] The temptation is ever present to project one's personal needs and aspirations into such a "generic" God, fashioning a deity that looks little different from oneself. See Stephen Prothero, *American Jesus: How the Son of God Became a National Icon* (New York: Farrar, Straus and Giroux, 2004).

used food and drink with those who are hungry. And this, too: the fast can also serve as nonviolent, peaceful protest in the presence of economic, political, or social affliction.

Consider the large group of women, led by Quakers, assembled in Washington, DC, in 1917 to lobby publicly for equal rights and the power to vote. Though President Wilson viewed them with benign regard, they were arrested and held in squalid prison quarters. Refusing to wear lice-ridden jail uniforms, they were beaten by the guards. Their protest of imprisonment and brutality was manifested in the refusal to eat: they began a collective fast that eventually led to their release. In 1932, Mahatma Gandhi, a student of Jesus's call to nonviolence in the Sermon on the Mount, began a hunger strike in opposition to the British colonial proposal to maintain a stratified class society with "untouchables" separated from the rest of the Indian population. "This is a God-given opportunity that has come to me," said Gandhi, "to offer my life as a sacrifice among the downtrodden." His refusal to eat led the British to change the separation of classes in civil legislation. In 1962 and 1964, young African Americans struggling for civil rights kept hunger strikes in Kentucky and Illinois—a protest against Jim Crow laws and government-sanctioned segregation of restaurants and grocery stores. In 1972, the Catholic farm worker and labor leader Cesar Chavez kept a "spiritual fast" as part of a protest in support of farm workers who labored in deplorable conditions. In the same year, he fasted in protest against legislation that prohibited boycotts and strikes by farm workers. In 1988, he fasted once more in protest against the use of pesticides in the fields in which farm workers labored—men and women experiencing a sharp increase in cancer diagnoses and the births of deformed infants. He was inspired, he said, by the ancient Catholic practice of fast and abstinence as well as Gandhi's nonviolent protests against injustice. In all these instances, the fast—the hunger strike—served as potent protest against economic, political, or social affliction. Thus, we find Quakers, Baptists, and Catholics refraining from food and drink: their fast, their strike, a plea for deliverance heard in every Eucharist: "Save us from the time of trial and deliver us from evil."

Promoting Limitations

The keeping of a fast never takes place in a vacuum. To claim that one is "giving up something for Lent" without awareness of the world in which one lives is simply naïve if not self-serving. Neither the celebration of the Eucharist nor the keeping of a eucharistic fast takes place in heaven but rather here on earth, in this world, where the many pray or plead for healing and nourishment: "Give us this day our daily bread." In this world, then—in this society marked so deeply by an addiction to consuming—one ethical dimension of eucharistic feasting might well be eucharistic fasting—that is, placing limits on the propensity to want more and more by channeling one's treasure, great or small, to the many in need. The ancient wisdom of the church juxtaposed fasting next to feasting—each one correcting the excesses of the other: too much or too little fasting; too much or too little feasting. Does the loss of fasting in actual practice among many Catholics and Anglicans and its historic absence among Protestants complement if not support a cultural mandate to overconsume? One wonders, however, if the invitation to question conspicuous wealth display and mass consumption, to place limits on the urge to have more and more, and to invest one's treasure—personal and parochial—in persons with manifest need is simply wishful thinking. Is it tantamount to economic heresy?

Much can be said of the Eucharist celebrated in the churches. A long and vital Christian tradition speaks of the Mass as the medicine of immortality—the promise of eternal life with God; as the forgiveness of one's sin; as a foretaste of the great feast in the new Jerusalem; as intimate encounter with the divine Lover—the Bridegroom who calls each seeking soul to himself; as the banquet of God's good creation set out for all who are hungry; as the sacrifice of praise and thanksgiving offered to God for the gift of salvation in Christ; as the bread of heaven and the cup of salvation. The Eucharist is neither a happy meal at which only the cheerful are welcomed nor a somber communion distributed in hushed tones to a procession of dour penitents. It is the encounter with the sacramental Christ who offers himself freely in bread and wine cup, his act of life-giving generosity. And, at the same time, it is the encounter with the One who fasted, who refrained from food and drink and counseled his followers to do the same. But that "doing the same" was and is an orientation to the other, the invitation to share from one's substance, rather than from one's excess, with those who have little food and drink. It is the invitation to set limits in a culture suffused with acquisitiveness, for, indeed, the setting of limits and the embrace of living in simplicity can serve as one's protest against an ideology that equates the amassing of quantities with quality of life.

In 1848, Elder Joseph Brackett wrote lyrics to accompany Shaker ritual dancing, a text familiar to many that begins with these words: "'Tis the gift to be simple, 'tis the gift to be free."[18] Sung within the context of emerging American industrialism that led to what Thorstein Veblen called "conspicuous consumption" and the growth of increasingly rigid

[18] Edward Andrews, *The Gift to Be Simple: Songs, Dances, and Rituals of the American Shakers* (New York: J.J. Augustin, 1940), 136. Here is the full text: "Tis the gift to be simple, 'tis the gift to be free / 'Tis the gift to come down where we ought to be, / And when we find ourselves in the place just right, / 'Twill be in the valley of love and delight. / When true simplicity is gained, / To bow and to bend we shan't be ashamed, / To turn, turn will be our delight, / Till by turning, turning we come'round right."

socioeconomic hierarchies, Brackett's lyric affirms setting limits and embracing a simple life clearly at odds with larger social trends. His text could be sung as a form of wishful thinking or nostalgia for an uncomplicated life in the midst of modernity's complexity. And it could be sung as protest of a troubling ideology that exerts considerable power in the churches.

The image of St. Francis comes to mind. Divesting himself of his father's luxurious clothing and thus his father's ambition to become a wealthy textile merchant and privileged leader in his city, Francis stood naked before the assembled citizens of Assisi until the bishop placed his cloak around the young man. In this moment of transition, of passage, so wrote the anthropologist Victor Turner, Francis, now divested of the ambition to acquire more and more, began to recognize and receive *the gifts of the earth*—the sun, the birds, the animals, the flowers, the dark soil of Umbria, the grain, and the grapevine—*as the true wealth* that comes from the hand of the benevolent Creator and his son who claimed no house, no land, no wealth as his own.[19] But this extravagant wealth was not to be hoarded by the few and conspicuously displayed in public. Rather, said the Poverello, earth's abundance—its water and olive oil, its bread and wine—is to be shared without favoritism among earth's children. Thus, set next to the astonishing and generous gift of the Eucharist—this one fragment of bread, this one sip of wine: enough but not too much—is the invitation to keep a fast so that one might offer food and drink to others, the invitation to set limitations on the acquisitiveness that appears "normal" in contemporary society.

---

[19] Victor Turner, "Passages, Margins, and Poverty: Religious Symbols of Communitas: Part One," *Worship* 46, no. 7 (August 1972): 411–412; "Part Two," *Worship* 46, no. 8 (October 1972): 491.

The liturgical hymn to Christ quoted by St. Paul in his letter to the church at Philippi sets forth a *kenotic* movement: "Though he was in the form of God, [Christ] did not regard equality with God as something to be exploited, but emptied himself" (Phil 2:6-7a). The hymn, sung in the liturgy, praises the relinquishment of one's privilege, the emptying of oneself for the sake of others. What the hymn then describes would be a position in life that the acquisitive, ambitious, and wealthy father of Francis—and a host of Christians and male church leaders accustomed to the privilege of their gender—could not imagine or would simply ignore: "[Christ] emptied himself taking the form of a slave . . . and being found in human form, he humbled himself and became obedient to the point of death—even death on a cross" (2:7-8). It was Dietrich Bonhoeffer, the German theologian martyred by the Nazi regime in 1945, who called Christian communities and their leaders to "see" the world and recognize its suffering "from below," and there discern the presence of the wounded and risen Christ:

> We have learned to see the great events of world history from below, from the perspective of the outcast, the suspects, the maltreated, the powerless, the oppressed, the reviled—in short, from the perspective of those who suffer. The important thing is . . . that we should come to look with new eyes . . . so that our perception of generosity, humanity, justice and mercy should become clearer [and] freer.[20]

If Christian ethics is less about obedience to the rule of law or discernment between right and wrong and more about living as disciples of Jesus Christ in the world, Francis's divestment of privilege and Bonhoeffer's call to see the world from the perspective of the outcast might well

---

[20] Dietrich Bonhoeffer, "After Ten Years," in *Letters and Papers from Prison* (New York: Touchstone, 1997), 17.

lead Christians to recognize the sacramental Christ as the servant who emptied himself—who poured out and broke open his life among the maltreated, the powerless, and the oppressed—a life marked by eucharistic gestures. What did he ask his disciples who were competing for positions of greatness? "Who is greater, the one who is at the table or the one who serves? Is it not the one at the table? But I am among you as one who serves" (Luke 22:27).

> Rise, O church, like Christ arisen,
> From this meal of love and grace;
> May we through such love envision
> Whose we are, and whose, our praise.
> Alleluia, alleluia: God, the wonder of our days.
>
> Service be our sure vocation;
> Courage be our daily breath;
> Mercy be our destination
> From this day and unto death.
> Alleluia, alleluia: Rise, O church a living faith.[21]

[21] Susan Palo Cherwien, *O Blessed Spring: Hymns of Susan Palo Cherwien* (Minneapolis: Augsburg Fortress, 1997), 36.

Chapter Eight

Three Homilies

The Kingdom of Heaven Is Like Yeast

Lectionary for Mass
Sixteenth Sunday in Ordinary Time Year A
Wisdom 12:13, 16-19; Psalm 86:5-6, 9-10, 15-16;
    Romans 8:26-27; Matthew 13:24-43 or 13:24-30

Evangelical Lutheran Worship Propers
Lectionary 17 in Year A
1 Kings 3:5-12; Psalm 119:129-36; Romans 8:26-39;
    Matthew 13:31-33, 44-52

Revised Common Lectionary
Proper 12 in Year A
Genesis 29:15-28 or 1 Kings 3:5-12; Psalm 105:1-11, 45b or
    Psalm 128 or Psalm 119:129-36; Romans 8:26-39;
    Matthew 13:31-33, 44-52

*The kingdom of heaven is like yeast that a woman took and
mixed in with three measures of flour until all of it was leavened.*
At first glance, this one sentence offers a simple image of
the kingdom of God with an equally simple message: the
kingdom grows in the world like yeast within flour. On

second glance, however, there is more to be discovered in this one sentence.

The gospels reveal the central message of Jesus as the presence of the kingdom or rule of God in human life and the invitation to live into and within that way of life. There is, however, another kingdom, another way of living in this world, one that sanctions discrimination, retribution, and violence; a kingdom in which some imagine they are superior to all others; in which some are seen as loyal insiders and everyone else as inferior outsiders; a kingdom in which "might" always makes "right." I ask you: is that kingdom, that way of life, the one in which you wish to dwell?

The kingdom of heaven is like yeast that a woman took and mixed with three measures of flour. Why does Jesus mention three and not two measures or one? Is it because we have heard this exact measurement before? For it is three measures of flour that Abraham uses to prepare bread for three angelic visitors; three measures that Hannah brings with her son, Samuel, to the house of the Lord. It is three measures that will be offered in the new temple described by Ezekiel and three measures of flour that will be baked into bread by the priests of the new temple.

It would seem, then, that mixing yeast into three measures, that is, a bushel of flour, would be a good thing, would it not? Well, except for this: the bread cakes prepared by Abraham were unleavened; and the offerings in the new temple were unleavened—no yeast! The celebration of Passover marks the removal of all yeast from the home and the Passover bread itself is unleavened. In other words, what is thought to be holy bread is yeast-free; what is profane, supposedly less than sacred, is yeasty. Why, then, does he endorse yeasty bread as an image of the kingdom?

But then the parable becomes more complicated when we recall the vision seen by the prophet Zechariah: The angel of the Lord showed me a basket with a heavy cover and once the cover was lifted, there I saw a woman sitting in three measures of flour. "This is Wickedness," said the attending angel pointing to the woman in the flour—for the woman in this vision was the god of war and destruction worshiped in the imperial kingdom of Babylon, that kingdom in which might always made right (Zech 5:5-11).

Thus to his listeners, Jesus's claim that the kingdom of heaven is like unholy yeast a woman mixes into three measures of flour would seem *utterly wrong*. Why would he compare the holiness of the kingdom of heaven to what could be perceived as unholy, unworthy of God? And so, would his listeners not be confused, even offended by this short parable? Or is it this: that he intends to shock his audience into unexpected awareness? Consider the actor in the parable, a woman. Did he not know and do we not know that in the history of the kingdoms of this world, in which some imagine they are always superior to others, a woman is viewed as dependent on a man, and if she rebels against her dependency and his control, should she not be pushed into submission, locked away, as it were, in a basket filled with flour? And yet here, with Jesus, she becomes nothing less than the astonishing image and agent—*the agent*—of the kingdom of heaven, an *utter reversal* of her status in the kingdoms of this world.

For you see: in the kingdom of heaven proclaimed by Jesus, what you and I may take for granted and accept out of custom just might be turned upside down. Why so? For this simple and tragic reason: the tendency to erect borders between insiders and outsiders, holy and unholy, is always present among us and around us; the tendency to imagine that one is superior to or at least a little bit better than others is always present, as can be seen in the institutions and invisible barriers that keep others outside, the barriers of human creation: the gated communities; the exclusive and excluding country clubs; the continued though illegal redlining of neighborhoods; the gerrymandering of congressional districts; the attempts to suppress voter registration; the discrimination directed at racial and sexual minorities; the churches that may say, "Welcome! Welcome!" but refuse the ethnic music and customs of people sitting in the pews.

Does this parable not point to Jesus who chooses to share life, *to share leavened, profane bread* with those who are perceived to be as unclean as yeast: to share life, not as their patronizing superior but as their compassionate equal? For it would seem that with Jesus there are no outsiders, no unclean, no inferiors who need to be walled off, redlined, excluded, or suppressed. In the kingdom of heaven, there is only the sharing of bread and life with anyone—*anyone*—who is hungry for God and God's gift of life.

The kingdom of heaven is in our midst; it comes to you and me without our bidding as the radical action of grace—that is, if we are able to receive it and then, as maturing Christians, cooperate with its yeasty power to grow within each of us and this parish. No wonder Jesus uses the wrong word—*leaven*—to speak of his followers, of you and me, as gloriously ordinary yeast, living with any and all who are perceived by the kingdoms of this world as unacceptable, as misfits, as not up to snuff, as not quite good enough. The kingdom of heaven is in our midst as we receive at this altar this woman's leavened and holy bread: a living, "edible" sign of the kingdom of heaven.

The only question is this: Shall we become what we eat?

I Am the Living Bread Come Down from Heaven

Lectionary for Mass
Twentieth Sunday in Ordinary Time Year B
Proverbs 9:1-6; Psalm 34:2-3, 4-5, 6-7; Ephesians 5:15-20;
    John 6:51-58

Evangelical Lutheran Worship Propers
Lectionary 20 in Year B
Proverbs 9:1-6; Psalm 34:9-14; Ephesians 5:15-20;
    John 6:51-58

Revised Common Lectionary
Proper 15 in Year B
1 Kings 2:10-12; 3:3-14 or Proverbs 9:1-6; Psalm 111 or
    Psalm 34:9-14; Ephesians 5:15-20; John 6:51-58

Michelle was a nursing student enrolled in my course on Medieval Christianity. Each day, she would arrive early for class and then spend some time cleaning her classroom table with a number of Handiwipes. Let's see, I thought to myself, a nursing student with a mild cleaning compulsion: no germ will ever be safe in your presence and no hospital patient will ever have to worry about a sterile environment if you are running the show. Honestly, I admired her energy, her commitment to nursing, and her singular devotion to doing the course work. And this, too: she drove me a little bit crazy. As a student of the sciences, she was eager to learn the "facts" about medieval Christianity. And as a student raised in a conservative evangelical church, she had learned to interpret the Bible in a "factual" manner, as if it were a scientific textbook—something it never claims to be.

Thus, as you might imagine, it was a challenge for this lovely and earnest young woman and many of her classmates to recognize that the language and ethos of religion is much less about giving one's assent to the "facts," and much more about living into a life with others, a life animated and shaped by the many images that emerge from both Scripture and that ongoing conversation we call tradition: images that enchant us, comfort us, challenge us, give us meaning, provoke our doubt, and animate our courage.

With others in the class, Michelle was surprised that medieval Christians could hold together diverse images of the central act of Christians, the Eucharist. "Isn't it just a reminder about the past?" she asked.

They were surprised, then, by reading Hildegard of Bingen, the medieval Benedictine mystic, who spoke of the Eucharist as God's free giving of "greenness," as heavenly rain for those who experience the dryness of loneliness, despair, or sin. They were perplexed, some even alarmed, when reading Julian of Norwich, the English anchorite, who claimed that Christ is our mother who nourishes us at the altar with life-giving drink from her ample breasts. They thought Francis of Assisi a little bit weird for preaching to a group of birds after he was run out of town and pelted with stones by the townspeople who were insulted when he preached that their disregard for the homeless who were hungry was disregard for Jesus, the Poor Man of Nazareth.

While the logical framework found in the theology of Thomas Aquinas, perhaps one of the world's greatest theologians, was appealing to many of the students, they wondered why such a bright man would be utterly devoted to the Eucharist, a devotion that inspired him to compose numerous hymns, especially the sequence for the Solemnity of Corpus Christi. They wondered about his insistence that the Eucharist is not, *is not*, merely a reminder of something from the past but rather an encounter in the present with the mystery of Christ, with the wounded and risen Christ who offers himself within the signs of bread and wine. They puzzled over his insistence that these words of Jesus— "I am the living bread that came down from heaven"—are neither a scientific statement about heaven's location nor an image, a metaphor, they could toss to the side simply because their sweet rational minds could not comprehend it. But here's the great irony: it was the self-identified atheist and social work major in the class who asked the question: "Were Francis of Assisi and Thomas Aquinas friends? Because it seems to me," he continued, "there might be some connection between the whole 'living bread' thing and the poor who are dying for living bread."

I wanted to shake his hand, pat him on the back, and kiss his broad atheist forehead (none of which I did), for he named, in his question, a dynamic that asks for your attention and mine. You see: bread has no other purpose than to nourish. It is not an object to be admired. Its one longing is to feed those who are hungry. Indeed, a certain violence must be done to bread in order for it do what it needs to do: it must be torn apart and then shared, for no mouth in this room or in any room on the planet is large enough to consume an entire loaf at once. Bread has no other purpose than to be broken apart and sustain those who are hungry.

It is of scandalous interest to me and I hope it is to you that we live in the nation that has the highest rate of obesity and the highest rate of food waste in the world. We are ranked lowest among all thirty-five industrialized nations in childhood hunger. One of every four children in our state lives with insufficient bread on a daily basis. "Does not the irony strike your heart," asked the Benedictine mystic Photina Rech, "that in a world filled with hungry people, Christ says, I AM LIVING BREAD?" Indeed, the One who gathers us at his altar and feeds us with his Body and Blood is nothing other than the Poor Man of Nazareth.

I wonder: What might he ask you and me to do with our gifts of daily bread?

To Whom Will All This Piled-Up Wealth of Yours Go?

Lectionary for Mass
Eighteenth Sunday in Ordinary Time Year C
Ecclesiastes 1:2; 2:21-23; Psalm 90:3-4, 5-6, 12-13, 14, 17;
    Colossians 3:1-5, 9-11; Luke 12:13-21

Evangelical Lutheran Worship Propers
Lectionary 18 in Year C
Ecclesiastes 1:2, 12-14; 2:18-23; Psalm 49:1-12;
    Colossians 3:1-11; Luke 12:13-21

Revised Common Lectionary
Proper 13 in Year C
Hosea 11:1-11 or Ecclesiastes 1:2, 12-14; 2:18-23;
    Psalm 107:1-9, 43 or Psalm 49:1-12; Colossians 3:1-11;
    Luke 12:13-21

This is what you and I need to grasp if we are to recognize the significance of Jesus's story for his largely impoverished audience who lived lives marked by subsistence, by living hand to mouth, day after day, never sure if there would be enough for tomorrow. In that ancient society most people—that is, poor working people—believed that everything in life existed in a limited supply. For those of us who have been raised in a capitalist system in which the unlimited growth of wealth is valued highly and in which one can gain wealth not through work but through investments, the notion that everything in life exists in a limited supply can be hard to grasp. But grasp it we must.

In the world in which Jesus lived and Luke wrote his gospel, in an agricultural economy in which a farmer or peasant relied on one small plot of land to sustain one's family from day to day, the small plot of land was the limited supply that could keep one alive, that is, barring a natural disaster, sickness, disability, or death. If anyone else experienced an increase in land, harvest, or wealth, either through work or through a windfall, that other person was usually perceived as a thief. In a world of limited supply, someone had to lose in order for someone to gain. And anyone who wanted more, who desired an increase in wealth or land or harvest (at the expense of others) would be motivated by greed, by the addictive hunger for more.

Thus we come to this parable. The rich man is rich because he is a landowner who owns far more than the vast majority of the population. He has experienced a bumper crop on his lands—but he does not mention that poor field workers were the ones who toiled in sowing, watering, weeding, and harvesting to produce such a crop. He does not mention they labored for a small daily wage that was sufficient only for today's food but not for tomorrow. Remember that for the laborer, food and drink is in limited supply, limited to the payment one receives at the end of the day: no contract, no union, no benefits package. "Oh, he's gained great wealth," think the many who work his land, "but gained it at our expense." He pays little to the many but increases wealth for himself alone.

Did you notice that the rich barn builder never mentions the word "we" or "us"? He says: "What should *I do*?" "*I will pull down* my barns . . . *I will store* all my grain . . . *I will say* to *my soul*: You have ample goods for many years." He is surrounded by scores of persons upon whom he is dependent, yet they are invisible to him; he is a child of God, yet the Creator and Owner of all things in heaven and on earth is absent from his ruminations. But, then, from his perspective—and perhaps from ours—he's simply a sharp businessman, committed to continued growth and investments that will pay off in the future while oblivious to the vast majority who live in a world of terribly limited supply.

My mother, ever the diplomat in our family, once said to me that she thought Jesus could use a lesson or two in manners: "He can sound so brash at times," she noted politely. "Testing people, calling them 'fools,' taking up a whip and entering the temple." Well, I think she was right on the brashness but I don't think Jesus was interested in a session on social etiquette with Miss Manners. Rather, I think he was and is profoundly concerned about what motivates our interactions with others, about who is visible and invisible to us, about who has worked with little to make the lives of others comfortable. Actually I am thinking about the women of color and the Ukrainian women immigrants who work in the assisted-living apartments where my mother lives: women who earn no more than minimal wage as they bring her medications, empty her bedside commode, help her take a shower, do her laundry, and make sure that she receives her daily food and drink. I think Jesus is profoundly concerned about who has access to what God creates for the well-being of *all* creatures, not just comfortable creatures among whom I count myself.

Never one to mince words, Jesus calls this supposedly sharp and profoundly self-invested investor a fool. Why so? Could it be that in the economy of God, any surplus is to be invested in other people rather than in projects whose only purpose is the accrual of more wealth for the few? Could it be that the economy of God is animated by an astonishing generosity and graciousness in a world whose original sin is the grasping hand, the grasping hand that wants more and more—a generosity that calls into question the ways in which we are taught by our culture to live with others? Could it be that the economy of God—so rarely discussed among Christians—invites you and me to ask how we as a parish, as households, as individuals might enlarge our generosity even when that enlarging includes loving protest of an economy that clearly benefits the few rather than the many?

I wonder if you have noticed this: that in the central ritual of Christians, the sharing of food and drink given to us by God, we engage in an unusual practice. The one who breaks bread—which is in limited supply at every Eucharist—needs to discern how large or small each piece will be so that everyone is able to partake in the one bread. The one who offers the cup relies on every communicant to take a measured sip so that there is sufficient for others gathered at the altar. The unemployed and comfortable retiree, the priest and the visitor, the child and the octogenarian all—*all*—receive the same amount of bread and wine. There is here an equitable sharing of God's gifts and thus the refusal of discrimination. In this most Holy Eucharist, you and I enter into and practice the economy of God's generosity, of God's richness toward us and all creatures. It should not surprise us, then, that the One who tells the parable seals with his body and blood the economy that longs to flourish in our lives, in our communities, and in our society.

The only question is this: Will our participation in the economy of heaven enliven our commitment to its flourishing here on earth?

Selected Bibliography

Balasuriya, Tissa. *Eucharist and Human Liberation.* Colombo, Sri Lanka: The Centre for Society and Religion, 1977.

Bellah, Robert, Richard Madsen, William Sullivan, Ann Swidler, and Steve Tipton. *Habits of the Heart: Individualism and Commitment in American Life.* Berkeley: University of California Press, 1996.

Benedict XVI. *The Sacrament of Charity: Sacramentum Caritatis.* Washington, DC: United States Conference of Catholic Bishops, 2007.

Bergant, Dianne. *The Earth Is the Lord's: The Bible, Ecology, and Worship.* Collegeville: Liturgical Press, 1998.

Boff, Leonardo, and Clodovis Boff. *Introducing Liberation Theology.* Translated by Paul Burns. Maryknoll: Orbis, 1987.

Bonhoeffer, Dietrich. *Letters and Papers from Prison.* New York: Touchstone, 1997.

The Book of Alternative Services of the Anglican Church of Canada. Toronto: Anglican Book Service, 1988.

Borg, Marcus. *Jesus: A New Vision: Spirit, Culture, and the Life of Discipleship.* New York: HarperCollins, 1991.

Brueggemann, Walter. *The Prophetic Imagination.* Second edition. Minneapolis: Fortress Press, 2001.

Carson, Rachel. *Silent Spring.* New York: Houghton Mifflin, 1962.

Carter, Warren. *Matthew and the Margins: A Sociopolitical and Religious Reading.* Maryknoll: Orbis, 2000.

Chauvet, Louis-Marie. *Symbol and Sacrament: A Sacramental Reinterpretation of Christian Existence.* Translated by Patrick Madigan and Madeleine Beaumont. Collegeville: Liturgical Press, 1995.

———. *Du symbolique au symbole: Essai sur les sacraments.* Paris: Éditions du Cerf, 1979.

Crossan, John Dominic. *God & Empire: Jesus Against Rome, Then and Now.* New York: HarperCollins, 2007.

———. *The Birth of Christianity: Discovering What Happened in the Years Immediately after the Execution of Jesus.* San Francisco: Harper-SanFrancisco, 1998.

Deiss, Lucien. *Springtime of the Liturgy: Liturgical Texts of the First Four Centuries.* Translated by Matthew J. O'Connell. Collegeville: Liturgical Press, 1979.

Dilasser, Maurice. *Symbols of the Church.* Translated by Mary Durkin, Madeleine Beaumont, and Caroline Morson. Collegeville: Liturgical Press, 1999.

Dillistone, F. W. *Traditional Symbols and the Contemporary World.* London: Epworth, 1973.

Eisen, Ute. *Women Officeholders in Early Christianity: Epigraphical and Literary Studies.* Translated by Linda Maloney. Collegeville: Liturgical Press, 2000.

Empereur, James, and Christopher Kiesling. *The Liturgy That Does Justice.* Collegeville: Liturgical Press, 1990.

A Eucharist Sourcebook. Edited by Robert Baker and Barbara Budde. Chicago: Liturgy Training Publications, 1999.

Fawcett, Thomas. *The Symbolic Language of Religion.* Minneapolis: Augsburg, 1971.

Fischer, Balthasar. *Signs, Words & Gestures.* Translated by Matthew O'Connell. New York: Pueblo, 1981.

Francis. *Laudato Si': On Care for Our Common Home.* Rome: Libreria Editrice Vaticana, 2015.

Guardini, Romano. *Sacred Signs.* Translated by Grace Branham. Wilmington: Michael Glazier, 1979.

Hanson, K. C., and Douglas E. Oakman. *Palestine in the Time of Jesus: Social Structures and Social Conflicts.* Second edition. Minneapolis: Fortress Press, 2008.

Hanson, K. C. "The Galilean Fishing Economy and the Jesus Tradition," in *Biblical Theology Bulletin* 27 (1997): 99–111.

Hellwig, Monika. *The Eucharist and the Hunger of the World.* Second edition. New York: Sheed and Ward, 1992.

Henderson, Frank, Stephen Larson, and Kathleen Quinn. *Liturgy, Justice, and the Reign of God: Integrating Vision and Practice.* Mahwah: Paulist Press, 1980.

Holman, Susan. *The Hungry Are Dying: Beggars and Bishops in Roman Cappadocia.* New York: Oxford University Press, 2001.

Hoppe, Leslie. *There Shall Be No Poor Among You: Poverty in the Bible.* Nashville: Abingdon Press, 2004.

Hovda, Robert. *Strong, Loving and Wise: Presiding in Liturgy.* Fifth edition. Collegeville: Liturgical Press, 1981.

Jewett, Robert. "Tenement Churches and Pauline Love Feasts," in *Quarterly Review* 14 (1994): 43–58.

Kahl, Sigurn. "The Religious Roots of Modern Poverty Policy: Catholic, Lutheran, and Reformed Protestant Traditions," in *Archives Européennes de Sociologie* 46, no. 1 (March 2005): 91–126.

Kardong, Terence. *Benedict's Rule: A Translation and Commentary.* Collegeville: Liturgical Press, 1996.

Karris, Robert. *Eating Your Way Through Luke's Gospel.* Collegeville: Liturgical Press, 2006.

Kavanagh, Aidan. *Elements of Rite: A Handbook of Liturgical Style.* Collegeville: Liturgical Press, 1990.

Lathrop, Gordon. *Holy Ground: A Liturgical Cosmology.* Minneapolis: Fortress Press, 2003.

————. *The Four Gospels on Sunday: The New Testament and the Reform of Christian Worship.* Minneapolis: Fortress Press, 2012.

Laverdiere, Eugene. *Dining in the Kingdom of God: The Origins of Eucharist according to Luke.* Chicago: Liturgy Training Publications, 2007.

————. *The Breaking of the Bread: The Development of the Eucharist according to Acts.* Chicago: Liturgy Training Publications, 2007.

Liturgy and Justice: To Worship God in Spirit and Truth. Edited by Anne Y. Koester. Collegeville: Liturgical Press, 2002.

Liturgy and Social Justice. Edited by Mark Searle. Collegeville: Liturgical Press, 1980.

Living No Longer for Ourselves: Liturgy and Justice in the Nineties. Edited by Kathleen Hughes and Mark R. Francis. Collegeville: Liturgical Press, 1991.

Lowery, Richard. *Sabbath and Jubilee.* St. Louis: Chalice Press, 2000.

Malina, Bruce J., and John Pilch. *Social Science Commentary on the Book of Acts.* Minneapolis: Fortress Press, 2008.

Malina, Bruce J., and Richard L. Rohrbaugh. *Social Science Commentary on the Synoptic Gospels.* Second edition. Minneapolis: Fortress Press, 2003.

Metz, Johann Baptist. "The Future in the Memory of Suffering," in *Faith in History and Society: Toward a Practical Fundamental Theology.* Translated by Matthew Ashley. New York: Crossroad Publishing, 1980.

Michel, Virgil. *The Social Question: Essays on Capitalism and Christianity.* Edited by Robert Spaeth. Collegeville: St. John's University, 1987.

————. *The Liturgy of the Church According to the Roman Rite.* New York: Macmillan, 1938.

————. "Liturgy as the Basis of Social Regeneration," in *Orate Fratres* 9, no. 12 (November 1935): 536–545.

Mick, Lawrence. *Liturgy and Ecology in Dialogue.* Collegeville: Liturgical Press, 1997.

Miles, Sara. *Jesus Freak: Feeding, Healing, Raising the Dead.* San Francisco: Jossey-Bass, 2010.

Myers, Ched. *The Biblical Vision of Sabbath Economics.* Ventura: Tell the Word, 2002.

Neyrey, Jerome. "Reader's Guide to Meals, Food and Table Fellowship in the New Testament," at https://www3.nd.edu/~jneyrey1/meals.html.

Norberg-Schulz, Christian. *Meaning in Western Architecture.* Revised edition. New York: Rizzoli, 1980.

Oakman, Douglas E. *Jesus, Debt and the Lord's Prayer.* Eugene: Wipf & Stock, 2014.

———. *The Political Aims of Jesus.* Minneapolis: Fortress Press, 2012.

———. *Jesus and the Peasants.* Eugene: Cascade Books, 2008.

Osiek, Carolyn, and Margaret MacDonald. *A Woman's Place: House Churches in Earliest Christianity.* Minneapolis: Fortress Press, 2005.

A Place at the Table. Edited by Peter Pringle. Philadelphia: Perseus Books/Public Affairs, 2013.

Rech, Photina. *Wine and Bread.* Translated by Heinz Kuehn. Chicago: Liturgy Training Publications, 1998.

Ringe, Sharon. *Jesus, Liberation, and the Biblical Jubilee.* Minneapolis: Fortress Press, 1985.

St. Basil the Great: On Social Justice. Translated by C. Paul Schroeder. Crestwood: St. Vladimir Seminary Press, 2009.

St. John Paul II. *As the Third Millennium Draws Near: Tertio Millennio Adveniente,* at https://w2.vatican.va/content/john-paul-ii/en/apost_letters/1994/documents/hf_jp-ii_apl_19941110_tertio-millennio-adveniente.html.

St. Leo the Great: Sermons. Vol. 93 of *The Fathers of the Church.* Translated by Jane Freeland and Agnes Conway. Washington, DC: Catholic University of America Press, 1996.

Sawicki, Marianne. "How Can Worship Be Contemporary?" in *What Is Contemporary Worship?* Edited by Gordon Lathrop. Minneapolis: Augsburg Fortress, 1995.

Schottroff, Luise, and Wolfgang Stegemann. *Jesus and the Hope of the Poor.* Translated by Matthew O'Connell. Eugene: Wipf & Stock, 2009.

Schwanke, Johannes. "Luther on Creation," in *Harvesting Martin Luther's Reflections on Theology, Ethics, and the Church.* Edited by Timothy J. Wengert. Grand Rapids: Eerdmans, 2004.

Schwartz-Nobel, Loretta. *Growing Up Empty: The Hunger Epidemic in America.* New York: Harper, 2001.

Sink, Susan. *The Art of The Saint John's Bible: The Complete Reader's Guide.* Collegeville: Liturgical Press, 2013.

Smith, Dennis E. *From Symposium to Eucharist: The Banquet in the Early Christian World.* Minneapolis: Fortress Press, 2003.

Snyder, Graydon. *Inculturation of the Jesus Tradition: The Impact of Jesus on Jewish and Roman Cultures.* London: Bloomsbury T & T Clark, 1999.

———. *ANTE PACEM: Archaeological Evidence of Church Life before Constantine.* Macon: Mercer University Press, 1991.

Stewart, Benjamin. *A Watered Garden: Christian Worship and Earth's Ecology.* Minneapolis: Augsburg Fortress, 2011.

Stringfellow, William. *The Politics of Spirituality.* Eugene: Wipf & Stock, 2013.

Torvend, Samuel. "Common Property for All Who Are Needy: Eucharistic Practice in the Midst of Economic Injustice," in *Politics and Economy of Liberation.* Vol. 3 of *Radicalizing Reformation.* Edited by Ulrich Duchrow and Martin Hoffmann. Berlin: LIT Verlag, 2015.

————. *Luther and the Hungry Poor: Gathered Fragments.* Minneapolis: Fortress Press, 2008.

————. *Daily Bread, Holy Meal: Opening the Gifts of Holy Communion.* Minneapolis: Augsburg Fortress, 2004.

Udoekpo, Michael Ufok. *Rethinking the Prophetic Critique of Worship in Amos 5 for Contemporary Nigeria and the USA.* Eugene: Pickwick Publications, 2017.

Veblen, Thorstein. *The Theory of the Leisure Class: An Economic Study of Institutions.* New York: Oxford University Press, 2009.

Weber, Max. *The Protestant Ethic and the Spirit of Capitalism.* Translated by Peter Baehr and Gordon Wells. New York: Penguin Books, 2002.

Index of Biblical Citations

Index of Subjects